THE DR. MAKARY DIET COOKBOOK

100+ Wholesome Recipes Inspired by Dr. Makary's Expertise to Prevent Health Blind Spots, Boost Wellness, and Elevate Your Wellbeing

30-Day Meal Plan Included

Elise Burns

Table Of Contents

Introduction

Overview of Health Blind Spots in Nutrition

In today's fast-paced world, many of us are unaware of the subtle yet significant ways in which our diet can affect our overall health. These unnoticed or overlooked issues are what we refer to as "health blind spots." Despite our best efforts to eat well and maintain a healthy lifestyle, misconceptions about nutrition, reliance on processed foods, and outdated dietary guidelines can lead to a range of health problems, such as fatigue, weight gain, and even chronic diseases.

The first step to overcoming these health blind spots is awareness. Many common beliefs about nutrition are outdated or overly simplified. For example, fat has long been considered the enemy, leading people to avoid it at all costs, yet not all fats are bad. Similarly, many are unaware of how refined carbohydrates can affect blood sugar levels, contributing to energy crashes and long-term health issues.

This book aims to bring these blind spots to light and help you develop a more nuanced and effective approach to nutrition. You'll discover how small adjustments to your daily eating habits can make a significant impact on your overall wellness. By addressing these blind spots, you can prevent common health issues, boost your energy, and improve your long-term health.

As we move forward, we'll unpack the key principles of Dr. Makary's approach to diet and wellness, which focuses on whole foods, balanced nutrition, and sustainable eating habits. This book will provide you with practical tools and delicious recipes that will empower you to make informed, science-backed decisions about what you eat, ensuring you nourish your body with the right nutrients while avoiding the common pitfalls that undermine health.

Together, we will explore the road to better health, free of misconceptions, and filled with satisfying, nutritious meals that fuel your body and mind.

Why Dr. Makary's Approach Works

Dr. Makary's approach to nutrition and wellness is grounded in both scientific research and practical, sustainable habits that make a lasting impact. His philosophy bypasses the confusion of fad diets and conflicting nutritional advice, offering a clear and effective path toward long-term health. By focusing on simplicity and evidence-based practices, his method is not only easy to follow but also highly effective in addressing modern dietary challenges.

At the heart of Dr. Makary's approach is a strong emphasis on whole, unprocessed foods. He advocates for the inclusion of fresh vegetables, fruits, lean proteins, whole grains, and healthy fats in the daily diet. Whole foods are the foundation of good health, providing the body with essential nutrients, vitamins, and minerals in their most natural and bioavailable forms. This focus on whole foods helps reduce inflammation, improve digestion, and provide sustained energy, which is crucial for maintaining overall wellness.

Dr. Makary's approach also stresses the importance of balanced macronutrients—carbohydrates, proteins, and fats—without vilifying any particular food group. Instead of promoting extreme dietary restrictions, he encourages the right combination of these macronutrients to create meals that are both satisfying and nourishing. This balance is key to stabilizing blood sugar, preventing energy crashes, and supporting long-term health goals like weight management and muscle maintenance.

What sets Dr. Makary's method apart is its grounding in evidence-based nutritional strategies. Every recommendation in this book is supported by rigorous scientific research. Rather than adhering to popular dietary myths, his approach is based on clinical studies that highlight the importance of nutrient-dense foods for disease prevention, energy optimization, and longevity. For example, his work debunks the misconception that all fats are harmful, and he clarifies the difference between complex and refined carbohydrates, guiding readers toward healthier, more informed choices.

Another critical aspect of Dr. Makary's philosophy is its focus on sustainability. Many modern diets are too restrictive and unsustainable in the long run, leading to frustration and failure. In contrast, Dr. Makary's approach is designed for the long haul. It is not about quick fixes or temporary changes but about adopting healthy habits that can be maintained for life. By emphasizing moderation, variety, and enjoyment of food, his method ensures that people can follow a nutritious eating plan without feeling deprived or overwhelmed.

Flexibility is another key strength of Dr. Makary's approach. He recognizes that every person's nutritional needs are unique, shaped by their individual health profiles, lifestyles, and goals. His method encourages adaptability, allowing individuals to tailor the principles to suit their specific circumstances. This personalized approach makes his guidance accessible to a wide range of people, regardless of their starting point or dietary preferences.

Finally, Dr. Makary's approach is not just about improving current health but also about preventing future health issues. His diet principles are proactive, focusing on the prevention of chronic diseases such as diabetes, heart disease, and even certain types of cancer. By adopting his nutrition strategies, individuals can work toward long-term vitality and wellbeing, creating a foundation for a healthier future.

This holistic, sustainable, and scientifically sound approach is what makes Dr. Makary's method truly effective. It empowers individuals to make informed, lasting changes to their diet and lifestyle, leading to better health, more energy, and a higher quality of life.

How to Use This Book

This book is crafted to serve as both a practical guide and a dependable resource that you can consult again and again. Whether you're just beginning to explore healthier eating habits or you're already knowledgeable about nutrition, *The Dr. Makary Diet Cookbook* is organized to provide you with clear, actionable steps toward your health goals.

The structure of the book starts with foundational knowledge, addressing common misconceptions about modern diets and explaining Dr. Makary's nutritional philosophy. These initial chapters aim to educate you on how certain foods can benefit or hinder your well-being. As you move forward, the focus shifts to incorporating whole foods, balancing macronutrients, and tailoring your dietary choices to suit your unique health needs.

At its core, this book is about practical application. It is not only filled with insights but also offers a collection of simple, flavorful recipes designed to make eating healthy enjoyable and sustainable. The recipes are grouped into categories like breakfasts, main courses, snacks, and desserts, making it easy to navigate and find meals that align with your routine and preferences. From quick dinners to meal-prep ideas and even nutritious treats, the book covers a wide range of options that fit into various lifestyles.

You can approach this book at your own pace. If you're new to these concepts, take time to explore the early chapters that explain the core principles. If you're more eager to start cooking, feel free to dive directly into the recipes. Each recipe is designed with flexibility in mind, offering tips for ingredient substitutions and adjustments based on what you have available or what best suits your tastes.

Dr. Makary's approach is adaptable, and this book is structured with that flexibility in mind. Whether you're following a vegetarian diet, avoiding gluten, or simply aiming to eat more whole foods, the recipes are versatile and can be customized to meet your needs. The goal is to make this book a daily tool in your kitchen, something that empowers you to make healthier choices without overwhelming you with complexity.

By integrating the knowledge and recipes found here into your everyday life, you can steadily build habits that support better health, increased energy, and a stronger sense of well-being. Use this book not only to prepare nourishing meals but also as a guide to understanding how food can transform your health in sustainable, long-lasting ways.

Chapter 1: Understanding Health Blind Spots in Nutrition

1. Kale & Lentil Detox Soup

This nourishing detox soup combines the earthy flavors of lentils and kale. It's packed with fiber, vitamins, and antioxidants, making it perfect for cleansing your system while keeping you full and satisfied.

Servings: 4 | **Prep Time**: 15 minutes | **Cooking Time**: 30 minutes

Ingredients:

- 1 cup green lentils, rinsed
- 1 bunch kale, stems removed and chopped
- 1 onion, finely chopped
- 2 carrots, diced
- 2 celery stalks, diced
- 3 cloves garlic, minced
- 1 can diced tomatoes (14 oz)
- 6 cups vegetable broth
- 1 tsp ground cumin
- 1 tsp turmeric
- 1 tbsp olive oil
- Salt and pepper to taste
- Lemon wedges for serving

Preparation Steps:

To begin, heat olive oil in a large pot over medium heat. Add the onion, garlic, carrots, and celery, sautéing until softened, which takes about 5-7 minutes. Stir in the cumin and turmeric, allowing the spices to release their aromas as they blend into the vegetables. After the spices are fragrant, add the lentils and diced tomatoes, stirring everything together before pouring in the vegetable broth. Bring the mixture to a boil, then reduce the heat to low and let it simmer for 20-25 minutes, or until the lentils are tender. In the final 5 minutes of cooking, stir in the chopped kale, allowing it to wilt and soften. Season the soup with salt and pepper to taste. Serve hot, with lemon wedges on the side for a fresh, tangy finish.

Nutritional Value (per serving):
Calories: 210 | Protein: 12g | Fat: 4g | Carbohydrates: 35g | Fiber: 12g | Vitamin A: 80% DV | Vitamin C: 60% DV | Iron: 25% DV

2. Quinoa & Avocado Salad with Citrus Dressing

This light and refreshing salad is packed with plant-based protein from quinoa and heart-healthy fats from avocado. The bright citrus dressing adds a zingy freshness, making it a perfect meal for lunch or a side dish for dinner.

Servings: 4 | **Prep Time**: 15 minutes | **Cooking Time**: 15 minutes

Ingredients:

- 1 cup quinoa, rinsed
- 1 ripe avocado, diced
- 1 cup cherry tomatoes, halved
- 1/2 red onion, thinly sliced
- 1/4 cup fresh cilantro, chopped
- 1/4 cup olive oil
- 2 tbsp lemon juice
- 2 tbsp lime juice
- 1 tsp honey or maple syrup
- Salt and pepper to taste

Preparation Steps:
Start by cooking the quinoa according to the package instructions, usually around 15 minutes. Once cooked, fluff the quinoa with a fork and let it cool. While the quinoa is cooling, prepare the dressing by whisking together olive oil, lemon juice, lime juice, honey, and a pinch of salt and pepper. In a large bowl, combine the cooled quinoa, diced avocado, cherry tomatoes, red onion, and cilantro. Pour the citrus dressing over the salad and toss gently to combine, being careful not to mash the avocado. Adjust seasoning with additional salt and pepper if necessary. Serve immediately for a fresh, zesty flavor.

Nutritional Value (per serving):
Calories: 250 | Protein: 6g | Fat: 18g | Carbohydrates: 22g | Fiber: 6g | Vitamin C: 45% DV | Iron: 10% DV | Potassium: 15% DV

3. Greek Yogurt & Berry Parfait

A simple yet nutritious parfait made with protein-rich Greek yogurt and antioxidant-packed berries. It's a perfect option for a quick breakfast or a healthy snack, providing a balance of protein, fiber, and natural sweetness.

Servings: 2 | **Prep Time**: 5 minutes | **Cooking Time**: None

Ingredients:

- 1 cup plain Greek yogurt
- 1/2 cup mixed berries (blueberries, strawberries, raspberries)
- 1/4 cup granola
- 1 tbsp honey
- 1 tbsp chia seeds (optional)

Preparation Steps:
Start by layering half of the Greek yogurt into two small bowls or glasses. Add a layer of mixed berries on top, followed by a sprinkle of granola and chia seeds if using. Drizzle honey over the layers for a touch of natural sweetness. Repeat the layers with the remaining yogurt, berries, and granola. Serve immediately and enjoy as a refreshing, nutritious treat.

Nutritional Value (per serving):
Calories: 220 | Protein: 12g | Fat: 5g | Carbohydrates: 28g | Fiber: 4g | Vitamin C: 25% DV | Calcium: 15% DV | Iron: 5% DV

4. Whole Wheat Zucchini Bread

This moist and wholesome zucchini bread is made with whole wheat flour and naturally sweetened with honey, making it a healthier alternative to traditional baked goods. Packed with fiber and nutrients, it's perfect for breakfast or as a snack.

Servings: 8 slices | **Prep Time**: 10 minutes | **Cooking Time**: 50 minutes

Ingredients:

- 1 1/2 cups whole wheat flour
- 1 tsp baking soda
- 1/2 tsp baking powder
- 1/2 tsp cinnamon
- 1/4 tsp salt
- 1/2 cup honey or maple syrup
- 1/4 cup olive oil or coconut oil
- 1 tsp vanilla extract
- 1 egg
- 1 1/2 cups grated zucchini
- 1/4 cup chopped walnuts (optional)

Preparation Steps:
Preheat the oven to 350°F (175°C) and grease a loaf pan. In a medium bowl, whisk together the flour, baking soda, baking powder, cinnamon, and salt. In a separate large bowl, mix the honey, oil, vanilla extract, and egg until smooth. Stir in the grated zucchini. Gradually fold the dry ingredients into the wet mixture, stirring just until combined. If using walnuts, gently fold them into the batter. Pour the batter into the prepared loaf pan and bake for about 50 minutes, or until a toothpick inserted into the center comes out clean. Allow the bread to cool in the pan for 10 minutes before transferring it to a wire rack to cool completely.

Nutritional Value (per slice):
Calories: 180 | Protein: 4g | Fat: 7g | Carbohydrates: 26g | Fiber: 3g | Vitamin A: 2% DV | Vitamin C: 6% DV | Iron: 8% DV

5. Hearty Vegetable and Barley Stew

This warm and filling stew features barley and a variety of colorful vegetables. It's rich in fiber, vitamins, and minerals, making it an excellent choice for a satisfying and nutritious meal.

Servings: 4 | **Prep Time**: 15 minutes | **Cooking Time**: 45 minutes

Ingredients:

- 1/2 cup pearl barley
- 1 onion, diced
- 2 carrots, sliced
- 2 celery stalks, diced
- 2 potatoes, cubed
- 1 zucchini, diced
- 1 can diced tomatoes (14 oz)
- 4 cups vegetable broth
- 1 tsp thyme
- 1 tsp paprika
- 1 tbsp olive oil
- Salt and pepper to taste
- Fresh parsley for garnish

Preparation Steps:
In a large pot, heat olive oil over medium heat and sauté the onion, carrots, and celery until softened, about 5 minutes. Add the diced potatoes, zucchini, and pearl barley, stirring to combine. Pour in the diced tomatoes and vegetable broth, then add thyme, paprika, salt, and pepper. Bring the mixture to a boil, then reduce the heat and let it simmer for 35-40 minutes, or until the barley is tender. Stir occasionally to prevent sticking. Adjust seasoning if necessary. Serve hot, garnished with fresh parsley for a burst of flavor.

Nutritional Value (per serving):
Calories: 220 | Protein: 6g | Fat: 5g | Carbohydrates: 40g | Fiber: 8g | Vitamin A: 70% DV | Vitamin C: 25% DV | Iron: 10% DV

6. Baked Sweet Potato with Almond Butter & Cinnamon

A simple, nutrient-dense snack or side dish, this baked sweet potato is topped with creamy almond butter and a sprinkle of cinnamon. Rich in fiber and healthy fats, it provides a satisfying balance of flavors and textures.

Servings: 2 | **Prep Time**: 5 minutes | **Cooking Time**: 45 minutes

Ingredients:

- 2 medium sweet potatoes
- 2 tbsp almond butter

- 1/2 tsp cinnamon
- 1 tsp honey or maple syrup (optional)

Preparation Steps:
Preheat the oven to 400°F (200°C). Wash the sweet potatoes thoroughly, then pierce them several times with a fork. Place the sweet potatoes on a baking sheet and bake for 45 minutes, or until tender when pierced with a fork. Once done, slice the sweet potatoes open lengthwise and top each with a tablespoon of almond butter. Sprinkle cinnamon on top and drizzle with honey or maple syrup if desired. Serve warm for a delicious and wholesome snack.

Nutritional Value (per serving):
Calories: 250 | Protein: 5g | Fat: 10g | Carbohydrates: 40g | Fiber: 7g | Vitamin A: 370% DV | Vitamin C: 10% DV | Iron: 6% DV

7. Chickpea & Spinach Stew

This hearty and comforting chickpea and spinach stew is packed with plant-based protein and fiber. Flavored with aromatic spices, it's a nutritious and filling dish that can be served on its own or with a side of whole grains.

Servings: 4 | **Prep Time**: 10 minutes | **Cooking Time**: 25 minutes

Ingredients:

- 2 tbsp olive oil
- 1 onion, diced
- 3 cloves garlic, minced
- 1 tsp cumin
- 1 tsp paprika
- 1/4 tsp cayenne pepper (optional)
- 1 can chickpeas (15 oz), drained and rinsed
- 1 can diced tomatoes (14 oz)
- 4 cups fresh spinach
- 2 cups vegetable broth
- Salt and pepper to taste

Preparation Steps:
In a large pot, heat olive oil over medium heat. Add the onion and garlic,

sautéing until softened and fragrant, about 5 minutes. Stir in the cumin, paprika, and cayenne pepper, cooking for another minute. Add the chickpeas, diced tomatoes, and vegetable broth, stirring to combine. Bring the mixture to a simmer and cook for 15 minutes to allow the flavors to meld. In the last 5 minutes of cooking, stir in the fresh spinach, letting it wilt. Season with salt and pepper to taste. Serve warm, optionally with a side of rice or quinoa.

Nutritional Value (per serving):
Calories: 210 | Protein: 7g | Fat: 9g | Carbohydrates: 28g | Fiber: 8g | Vitamin A: 70% DV | Vitamin C: 35% DV | Iron: 15% DV

8. Apple Cinnamon Oatmeal

This comforting bowl of oatmeal is infused with the sweet and warm flavors of apple and cinnamon. It's a fiber-rich and heart-healthy breakfast that will keep you full and energized throughout the morning.

Servings: 2 | **Prep Time**: 5 minutes | **Cooking Time**: 10 minutes

Ingredients:

- 1 cup rolled oats
- 1 1/2 cups almond milk (or any milk of choice)
- 1 apple, peeled and diced
- 1/2 tsp cinnamon
- 1 tbsp honey or maple syrup (optional)
- 2 tbsp chopped walnuts (optional)

Preparation Steps:
In a small saucepan, combine the rolled oats, almond milk, diced apple, and cinnamon. Cook over medium heat, stirring occasionally, until the oats are soft and the apple pieces are tender, about 8-10 minutes. If the mixture becomes too thick, add a little more milk to reach your desired consistency. Stir in honey or maple syrup for added sweetness, if desired. Serve the oatmeal warm, topped with chopped walnuts for an extra crunch.

Nutritional Value (per serving):
Calories: 280 | Protein: 6g | Fat: 8g | Carbohydrates: 48g | Fiber: 6g | Vitamin C: 10% DV | Calcium: 20% DV | Iron: 10% DV

9. Spinach & Egg Breakfast Muffins

These protein-packed breakfast muffins are loaded with spinach and eggs, making them a convenient grab-and-go option for busy mornings. They're rich in protein and nutrients, providing a great start to your day.

Servings: 6 muffins | **Prep Time**: 10 minutes | **Cooking Time**: 20 minutes

Ingredients:

- 6 large eggs
- 1/2 cup spinach, finely chopped
- 1/4 cup red bell pepper, diced
- 1/4 cup onion, diced
- 1/4 cup shredded cheese (optional)
- Salt and pepper to taste
- Cooking spray

Preparation Steps:
Preheat the oven to 350°F (175°C) and spray a muffin tin with cooking spray. In a bowl, whisk together the eggs, then stir in the spinach, red bell pepper, onion, and shredded cheese if using. Season with salt and pepper to taste. Pour the egg mixture evenly into the prepared muffin tin, filling each cup about three-quarters full. Bake for 18-20 minutes, or until the eggs are set and lightly golden. Allow the muffins to cool for a few minutes before removing them from the tin. Serve warm or store in the fridge for up to 3 days for a quick breakfast.

Nutritional Value (per muffin):
Calories: 80 | Protein: 7g | Fat: 5g | Carbohydrates: 2g | Fiber: 1g | Vitamin A: 20% DV | Calcium: 6% DV | Iron: 4% DV

10. Roasted Tomato Basil Soup

This classic roasted tomato basil soup is rich in flavor and packed with nutrients. Roasting the tomatoes brings out their natural sweetness, while fresh basil adds a burst of freshness to this comforting dish.

Servings: 4 | **Prep Time**: 10 minutes | **Cooking Time**: 40 minutes

Ingredients:

- 6 large tomatoes, halved
- 1 onion, quartered
- 3 cloves garlic, peeled
- 2 tbsp olive oil
- 4 cups vegetable broth
- 1/4 cup fresh basil leaves, chopped
- Salt and pepper to taste
- 1 tsp balsamic vinegar (optional)

Preparation Steps:
Preheat the oven to 400°F (200°C). Place the halved tomatoes, onion, and garlic on a baking sheet, drizzle with olive oil, and season with salt and pepper. Roast for 25-30 minutes, or until the tomatoes are soft and caramelized. Once the vegetables are roasted, transfer them to a blender or food processor, and blend until smooth. Pour the blended mixture into a large pot, adding the vegetable broth, and bring to a simmer over medium heat. Stir in the chopped basil and balsamic vinegar for added depth of flavor, adjusting the seasoning as needed. Serve hot with a drizzle of olive oil or a sprinkle of fresh basil.

Nutritional Value (per serving):
Calories: 180 | Protein: 3g | Fat: 9g | Carbohydrates: 23g | Fiber: 5g | Vitamin A: 50% DV | Vitamin C: 60% DV | Iron: 10% DV

Chapter 2: The Foundation of The Dr. Makary Diet

11. Roasted Butternut Squash & Pomegranate Salad

This vibrant and nutritious salad combines the sweetness of roasted butternut squash with the tangy burst of fresh pomegranate seeds. It's a perfect balance of flavors, packed with fiber, vitamins, and antioxidants.

Servings: 4 | **Prep Time**: 10 minutes | **Cooking Time**: 30 minutes

Ingredients:

- 1 medium butternut squash, peeled and cubed
- 2 tbsp olive oil
- Salt and pepper to taste
- 1/2 cup pomegranate seeds
- 1/4 cup feta cheese, crumbled (optional)
- 1/4 cup fresh parsley, chopped
- 1 tbsp balsamic vinegar
- 1 tbsp honey or maple syrup

Preparation Steps:
Preheat the oven to 400°F (200°C). Toss the cubed butternut squash with olive oil, salt, and pepper, then spread it on a baking sheet. Roast for 25-30 minutes, or until tender and lightly browned, stirring halfway through. While the squash is roasting, prepare the dressing by whisking together balsamic vinegar and honey. Once the squash is done, let it cool slightly, then toss it in a large bowl with pomegranate seeds, parsley, and crumbled feta if using. Drizzle the salad with the balsamic-honey dressing, toss to combine, and serve warm or at room temperature.

Nutritional Value (per serving):
Calories: 230 | Protein: 4g | Fat: 9g | Carbohydrates: 35g | Fiber: 6g | Vitamin A: 200% DV | Vitamin C: 40% DV | Calcium: 10% DV

12. Grilled Vegetable Platter with Garlic Tahini

This colorful platter of grilled vegetables paired with a rich garlic tahini sauce makes for a nutrient-dense, flavorful dish that can be enjoyed as a side or a main course.

Servings: 4 | **Prep Time**: 15 minutes | **Cooking Time**: 20 minutes

Ingredients:

- 1 zucchini, sliced
- 1 eggplant, sliced
- 1 red bell pepper, sliced
- 1 yellow bell pepper, sliced
- 1 red onion, quartered
- 2 tbsp olive oil
- Salt and pepper to taste
- 1/4 cup tahini
- 1 clove garlic, minced
- 1 tbsp lemon juice
- 1 tbsp water (as needed to thin the sauce)

Preparation Steps:
Preheat a grill or grill pan over medium-high heat. In a large bowl, toss the sliced vegetables with olive oil, salt, and pepper until evenly coated. Grill the vegetables for 3-4 minutes on each side, or until charred and tender. Meanwhile, prepare the garlic tahini sauce by whisking together the tahini, minced garlic, lemon juice, and water (adding more water as needed to achieve a smooth, pourable consistency). Once the vegetables are grilled, arrange them on a platter and drizzle with the garlic tahini sauce. Serve immediately as a side dish or a light meal.

Nutritional Value (per serving):
Calories: 210 | Protein: 4g | Fat: 16g | Carbohydrates: 15g | Fiber: 6g | Vitamin A: 15% DV | Vitamin C: 60% DV | Calcium: 6% DV

13. Grilled Chicken & Farro Power Bowl

This satisfying power bowl features grilled chicken served over hearty farro, combined with nutrient-rich vegetables and a light lemon dressing. It's a well-balanced meal that provides plenty of protein, fiber, and healthy fats.

Servings: 4 | **Prep Time**: 15 minutes | **Cooking Time**: 30 minutes

Ingredients:

- 1 cup farro, rinsed
- 2 boneless, skinless chicken breasts
- 2 tbsp olive oil, divided
- 1 cucumber, diced
- 1 cup cherry tomatoes, halved
- 1/4 red onion, thinly sliced
- 2 tbsp fresh parsley, chopped
- 2 tbsp lemon juice
- Salt and pepper to taste

Preparation Steps:
Cook the farro according to package instructions, then set aside to cool slightly. Meanwhile, heat 1 tablespoon of olive oil in a grill pan over medium-high heat. Season the chicken breasts with salt and pepper, then grill for 6-7 minutes on each side, or until cooked through. Remove from the grill and allow the chicken to rest for a few minutes before slicing. In a large bowl, combine the cooked farro, diced cucumber, cherry tomatoes, red onion, and parsley. Drizzle with the remaining olive oil and lemon juice, tossing to combine. Serve the farro salad topped with grilled chicken slices.

Nutritional Value (per serving):
Calories: 350 | Protein: 25g | Fat: 12g | Carbohydrates: 40g | Fiber: 7g | Vitamin C: 25% DV | Iron: 10% DV | Calcium: 4% DV

14. Baked Salmon with Herb Quinoa

This healthy dish pairs perfectly baked salmon with a side of fluffy herb-infused quinoa, offering a nutritious balance of omega-3s, lean protein, and whole grains.

Servings: 4 | **Prep Time**: 10 minutes | **Cooking Time**: 25 minutes

Ingredients:

- 4 salmon fillets (4-6 oz each)
- 1 tbsp olive oil
- Salt and pepper to taste
- 1 cup quinoa, rinsed
- 2 cups vegetable broth
- 2 tbsp fresh parsley, chopped
- 1 tbsp fresh dill, chopped
- 1 tbsp lemon juice

Preparation Steps:
Preheat the oven to 400°F (200°C). Place the salmon fillets on a baking sheet lined with parchment paper, drizzle with olive oil, and season with salt and pepper. Bake for 15-20 minutes, or until the salmon is flaky and cooked through. Meanwhile, cook the quinoa in vegetable broth according to package instructions, then fluff with a fork and stir in parsley, dill, and lemon juice. Serve the salmon fillets over the herb quinoa, garnished with an additional sprinkle of fresh herbs if desired.

Nutritional Value (per serving):
Calories: 380 | Protein: 32g | Fat: 15g | Carbohydrates: 26g | Fiber: 4g | Vitamin A: 8% DV | Vitamin C: 15% DV | Iron: 12% DV

15. Spring Asparagus and Pea Risotto

This creamy risotto celebrates the fresh flavors of spring with tender asparagus and sweet peas. It's a comforting yet healthy meal that's rich in fiber and antioxidants.

Servings: 4 | **Prep Time**: 10 minutes | **Cooking Time**: 35 minutes

Ingredients:

- 1 cup arborio rice
- 1 tbsp olive oil

- 1 small onion, finely chopped
- 1 clove garlic, minced
- 4 cups vegetable broth, warmed
- 1/2 cup dry white wine (optional)
- 1 cup asparagus, chopped
- 1/2 cup green peas (fresh or frozen)
- 1/4 cup grated Parmesan (optional)
- Salt and pepper to taste

Preparation Steps:

In a large pan, heat olive oil over medium heat. Add the chopped onion and garlic, cooking until softened, about 5 minutes. Stir in the arborio rice, coating it with the oil, and cook for another 2 minutes. Pour in the white wine (if using) and stir until absorbed. Gradually add the warm vegetable broth, one ladle at a time, stirring constantly and allowing each addition to be absorbed before adding more. After about 20 minutes, when the rice is almost tender, stir in the asparagus and peas. Cook for another 5-7 minutes, or until the vegetables are tender and the risotto is creamy. Stir in Parmesan (if using) and season with salt and pepper to taste. Serve immediately.

Nutritional Value (per serving):

Calories: 320 | Protein: 8g | Fat: 8g | Carbohydrates: 50g | Fiber: 5g | Vitamin A: 15% DV | Vitamin C: 30% DV | Iron: 10% DV

16. Autumn Roasted Root Vegetables

This colorful mix of roasted root vegetables makes a perfect side dish or light main meal. The vegetables are caramelized to perfection, enhancing their natural sweetness, and seasoned with fragrant herbs for added depth.

Servings: 4 | **Prep Time**: 10 minutes | **Cooking Time**: 40 minutes

Ingredients:

- 2 carrots, peeled and cut into chunks
- 2 parsnips, peeled and cut into chunks
- 1 sweet potato, peeled and cubed
- 1 red onion, quartered
- 2 tbsp olive oil

- 1 tsp dried thyme
- 1 tsp dried rosemary
- Salt and pepper to taste

Preparation Steps:
Preheat the oven to 400°F (200°C). In a large bowl, toss the carrots, parsnips, sweet potato, and red onion with olive oil, thyme, rosemary, salt, and pepper until evenly coated. Spread the vegetables in a single layer on a baking sheet. Roast for 35-40 minutes, stirring halfway through, until the vegetables are tender and caramelized. Serve warm, garnished with fresh herbs if desired.

Nutritional Value (per serving):
Calories: 200 | Protein: 3g | Fat: 9g | Carbohydrates: 30g | Fiber: 6g | Vitamin A: 180% DV | Vitamin C: 20% DV | Iron: 6% DV

17. Moroccan Spiced Couscous with Vegetables

A fragrant and flavorful dish, this Moroccan-inspired couscous is paired with an array of vegetables and seasoned with aromatic spices like cumin and cinnamon.

Servings: 4 | **Prep Time**: 10 minutes | **Cooking Time**: 20 minutes

Ingredients:

- 1 cup couscous
- 1 tbsp olive oil
- 1 zucchini, diced
- 1 carrot, diced
- 1/2 red bell pepper, diced
- 1/2 tsp ground cumin
- 1/2 tsp ground cinnamon
- 1/4 tsp turmeric
- 1/4 cup raisins
- 1/4 cup slivered almonds (optional)
- 2 cups vegetable broth
- Salt and pepper to taste

Preparation Steps:
In a medium saucepan, bring the vegetable broth to a boil. Stir in the couscous,

cover, and remove from heat. Let sit for 5 minutes, then fluff with a fork. In a skillet, heat olive oil over medium heat. Add the zucchini, carrot, and red bell pepper, and sauté for 5-7 minutes until the vegetables are tender. Stir in the cumin, cinnamon, and turmeric, and cook for another minute. Add the sautéed vegetables, raisins, and almonds (if using) to the fluffed couscous and toss to combine. Season with salt and pepper to taste and serve warm.

Nutritional Value (per serving):
Calories: 250 | Protein: 6g | Fat: 8g | Carbohydrates: 40g | Fiber: 4g | Vitamin A: 50% DV | Vitamin C: 30% DV | Iron: 10% DV

18. Red Lentil Curry with Basmati Rice

This comforting red lentil curry is packed with plant-based protein and bold spices, served over fluffy basmati rice. It's a wholesome and warming dish that's perfect for any time of the year.

Servings: 4 | **Prep Time**: 10 minutes | **Cooking Time**: 30 minutes

Ingredients:

- 1 cup red lentils, rinsed
- 1 onion, diced
- 2 cloves garlic, minced
- 1 tbsp olive oil
- 1 tbsp curry powder
- 1 tsp ground turmeric
- 1 can diced tomatoes (14 oz)
- 2 cups vegetable broth
- 1/2 cup coconut milk
- 1 cup basmati rice, cooked according to package instructions
- Fresh cilantro for garnish
- Salt and pepper to taste

Preparation Steps:
In a large pot, heat olive oil over medium heat. Sauté the onion and garlic for 5 minutes, until softened. Stir in the curry powder and turmeric, cooking for another minute until fragrant. Add the red lentils, diced tomatoes, and vegetable broth. Bring to a boil, then reduce the heat and let it simmer for 20-

25 minutes, or until the lentils are tender. Stir in the coconut milk, season with salt and pepper, and simmer for another 5 minutes. Serve the curry over cooked basmati rice, garnished with fresh cilantro.

Nutritional Value (per serving):
Calories: 350 | Protein: 12g | Fat: 10g | Carbohydrates: 55g | Fiber: 10g | Vitamin A: 15% DV | Vitamin C: 20% DV | Iron: 20% DV

19. Quinoa Stuffed Bell Peppers

These vibrant bell peppers are stuffed with a delicious quinoa and vegetable mixture, making them a nutrient-dense and satisfying plant-based meal.

Servings: 4 | **Prep Time**: 15 minutes | **Cooking Time**: 30 minutes

Ingredients:

- 4 large bell peppers, tops cut off and seeds removed
- 1 cup quinoa, rinsed
- 1 tbsp olive oil
- 1 zucchini, diced
- 1/2 cup cherry tomatoes, halved
- 1/4 cup black beans, drained and rinsed
- 1/4 cup corn kernels
- 1 tsp ground cumin
- 1 tsp paprika
- 1 cup vegetable broth
- Salt and pepper to taste
- Fresh parsley for garnish

Preparation Steps:
Preheat the oven to 375°F (190°C). In a medium saucepan, bring the vegetable broth to a boil and add the quinoa. Lower the heat, cover, and simmer for 15 minutes or until the quinoa is cooked. In a skillet, heat the olive oil over medium heat and sauté the zucchini, cherry tomatoes, black beans, and corn for 5-7 minutes. Stir in the cumin, paprika, salt, and pepper, then add the cooked quinoa and toss to combine. Stuff the bell peppers with the quinoa mixture and place them in a baking dish. Bake for 20-25 minutes until the peppers are tender. Garnish with fresh parsley and serve.

Nutritional Value (per serving):
Calories: 280 | Protein: 8g | Fat: 8g | Carbohydrates: 45g | Fiber: 8g | Vitamin A: 90% DV | Vitamin C: 150% DV | Iron: 15% DV

20. Grilled Lemon Chicken with Brown Rice & Broccoli

This simple yet flavorful grilled lemon chicken is paired with hearty brown rice and steamed broccoli, creating a balanced and satisfying meal packed with protein and fiber.

Servings: 4 | **Prep Time**: 10 minutes | **Cooking Time**: 25 minutes

Ingredients:

- 2 boneless, skinless chicken breasts, halved lengthwise
- 1 tbsp olive oil
- 1 lemon, juiced
- 1 tsp garlic powder
- Salt and pepper to taste
- 1 cup brown rice, cooked according to package instructions
- 2 cups broccoli florets, steamed

Preparation Steps:
In a small bowl, whisk together the olive oil, lemon juice, garlic powder, salt, and pepper. Coat the chicken breasts with the marinade and let sit for 10 minutes. Preheat a grill or grill pan over medium-high heat. Grill the chicken for 5-6 minutes on each side, or until fully cooked through. Serve the grilled chicken alongside cooked brown rice and steamed broccoli for a balanced and delicious meal.

Nutritional Value (per serving):
Calories: 350 | Protein: 30g | Fat: 10g | Carbohydrates: 35g | Fiber: 5g | Vitamin C: 80% DV | Calcium: 6% DV | Iron: 10% DV

Chapter 3: Breakfasts to Start Your Day Right

21. Scrambled Eggs with Spinach & Smoked Salmon

This protein-rich breakfast combines fluffy scrambled eggs with nutrient-packed spinach and flavorful smoked salmon. It's a great way to fuel your day with essential vitamins and healthy fats.

Servings: 2 | **Prep Time**: 5 minutes | **Cooking Time**: 10 minutes

Ingredients:

- 4 large eggs
- 1/4 cup milk (optional)
- 1 cup fresh spinach, chopped
- 2 oz smoked salmon, chopped
- 1 tbsp butter or olive oil
- Salt and pepper to taste
- Fresh chives for garnish (optional)

Preparation Steps:
In a small bowl, whisk the eggs with the milk (if using) and season with salt and pepper. Heat the butter or olive oil in a non-stick skillet over medium heat. Add the chopped spinach and sauté until wilted, about 1-2 minutes. Pour in the egg mixture and stir gently, cooking until the eggs are just set but still soft. Remove from heat and stir in the smoked salmon. Serve immediately, garnished with fresh chives if desired.

Nutritional Value (per serving):
Calories: 250 | Protein: 22g | Fat: 17g | Carbohydrates: 4g | Fiber: 1g | Vitamin A: 60% DV | Vitamin C: 10% DV | Iron: 10% DV

22. Veggie Omelet with Mushrooms and Peppers

This veggie-packed omelet is filled with mushrooms, bell peppers, and onions, making it a flavorful and nutrient-dense option for a healthy start to your day.

Servings: 1 | **Prep Time**: 5 minutes | **Cooking Time**: 10 minutes

Ingredients:

- 2 large eggs
- 1/4 cup mushrooms, sliced
- 1/4 cup bell peppers, diced
- 1/4 small onion, diced
- 1 tbsp olive oil
- Salt and pepper to taste
- Fresh parsley for garnish (optional)

Preparation Steps:
In a small bowl, whisk the eggs and season with salt and pepper. Heat the olive oil in a skillet over medium heat. Add the mushrooms, bell peppers, and onions, and sauté for 4-5 minutes until softened. Pour the eggs over the sautéed vegetables, letting them cook undisturbed for 1-2 minutes. Once the eggs begin to set, gently fold the omelet in half and cook for another minute. Slide the omelet onto a plate and garnish with fresh parsley if desired.

Nutritional Value (per serving):
Calories: 200 | Protein: 12g | Fat: 15g | Carbohydrates: 6g | Fiber: 2g | Vitamin A: 20% DV | Vitamin C: 40% DV | Iron: 6% DV

23. Almond Flour Pancakes with Chia Seeds

These fluffy almond flour pancakes are a gluten-free and protein-rich option, enhanced with chia seeds for an extra boost of fiber and omega-3 fatty acids.

Servings: 2 | **Prep Time**: 5 minutes | **Cooking Time**: 10 minutes

Ingredients:

- 1 cup almond flour
- 1 tbsp chia seeds
- 1 tsp baking powder
- 2 large eggs
- 1/4 cup almond milk (or any milk of choice)
- 1 tsp vanilla extract

- 1 tbsp maple syrup (optional)
- Butter or oil for cooking

Preparation Steps:
In a mixing bowl, whisk together the almond flour, chia seeds, and baking powder. In a separate bowl, whisk the eggs, almond milk, vanilla extract, and maple syrup (if using). Pour the wet ingredients into the dry mixture and stir until just combined. Heat a non-stick skillet over medium heat and lightly grease it with butter or oil. Pour 2-3 tablespoons of batter onto the skillet for each pancake. Cook for 2-3 minutes on each side, or until golden brown. Serve warm with your favorite toppings.

Nutritional Value (per serving):
Calories: 320 | Protein: 12g | Fat: 25g | Carbohydrates: 12g | Fiber: 6g | Vitamin E: 30% DV | Calcium: 10% DV | Iron: 8% DV

24. Overnight Oats with Berries and Flaxseeds

This easy and nutritious breakfast is perfect for busy mornings. The oats soak overnight, creating a creamy texture, while the berries and flaxseeds add fiber and antioxidants.

Servings: 1 | **Prep Time**: 5 minutes | **Cooking Time**: None (overnight soak)

Ingredients:

- 1/2 cup rolled oats
- 1/2 cup almond milk (or any milk of choice)
- 1/4 cup mixed berries (blueberries, strawberries, raspberries)
- 1 tbsp flaxseeds
- 1 tsp honey or maple syrup (optional)
- 1/4 tsp cinnamon

Preparation Steps:
In a mason jar or small bowl, combine the rolled oats, almond milk, flaxseeds, and cinnamon. Stir well, then top with mixed berries and drizzle with honey or maple syrup if desired. Cover and refrigerate overnight. In the morning, give it a stir and enjoy straight from the jar or transfer it to a bowl for serving.

Nutritional Value (per serving):
Calories: 220 | Protein: 6g | Fat: 7g | Carbohydrates: 35g | Fiber: 8g | Vitamin C: 10% DV | Calcium: 15% DV | Iron: 10% DV

25. Apple Cinnamon Quinoa Breakfast Bowl

This warm and hearty quinoa breakfast bowl is flavored with cinnamon and apples, offering a nutritious and protein-rich alternative to traditional oatmeal.

Servings: 2 | **Prep Time**: 5 minutes | **Cooking Time**: 15 minutes

Ingredients:

- 1/2 cup quinoa, rinsed
- 1 cup almond milk (or any milk of choice)
- 1 apple, peeled and diced
- 1/2 tsp cinnamon
- 1 tbsp honey or maple syrup (optional)
- 2 tbsp chopped walnuts (optional)

Preparation Steps:
In a small saucepan, combine the rinsed quinoa, almond milk, diced apple, and cinnamon. Bring to a simmer over medium heat, then reduce the heat to low and cook for 12-15 minutes, or until the quinoa is tender and the liquid is absorbed. Stir in honey or maple syrup for added sweetness if desired. Serve the quinoa warm, topped with chopped walnuts for a satisfying crunch.

Nutritional Value (per serving):
Calories: 280 | Protein: 7g | Fat: 9g | Carbohydrates: 45g | Fiber: 6g | Vitamin C: 10% DV | Calcium: 20% DV | Iron: 10% DV

26. Whole Grain Toast with Avocado and Hemp Seeds

This simple and nutrient-dense breakfast option features creamy avocado spread on whole grain toast, topped with hemp seeds for added protein and omega-3 fatty acids.

Servings: 1 | **Prep Time**: 5 minutes | **Cooking Time**: None

Ingredients:

- 1 slice whole grain bread, toasted
- 1/2 ripe avocado, mashed
- 1 tsp hemp seeds
- Salt and pepper to taste
- A squeeze of lemon juice (optional)

Preparation Steps:
Spread the mashed avocado evenly over the toasted whole grain bread. Sprinkle with hemp seeds, then season with salt and pepper to taste. If desired, add a squeeze of fresh lemon juice for extra flavor. Serve immediately for a quick, nutritious breakfast.

Nutritional Value (per serving):
Calories: 210 | Protein: 6g | Fat: 14g | Carbohydrates: 18g | Fiber: 6g | Vitamin E: 10% DV | Potassium: 10% DV | Iron: 8% DV

27. Green Smoothie with Kale, Banana & Almond Butter

This energizing green smoothie is packed with kale, banana, and almond butter, providing a great balance of vitamins, healthy fats, and protein to start your day.

Servings: 2 | **Prep Time**: 5 minutes | **Cooking Time**: None

Ingredients:

- 1 cup kale, chopped
- 1 banana, sliced
- 1 tbsp almond butter
- 1 cup almond milk (or any milk of choice)
- 1 tsp honey or maple syrup (optional)
- 1/2 cup ice cubes

Preparation Steps:
In a blender, combine the kale, banana, almond butter, almond milk, and ice cubes. Blend until smooth, adding more almond milk if needed to reach your desired consistency. Taste and add honey or maple syrup if you prefer a sweeter smoothie. Pour into two glasses and serve immediately.

Nutritional Value (per serving):
Calories: 220 | Protein: 5g | Fat: 11g | Carbohydrates: 28g | Fiber: 5g | Vitamin A: 60% DV | Vitamin C: 70% DV | Calcium: 15% DV

28. Antioxidant-Rich Blueberry & Chia Smoothie

This delicious smoothie is packed with antioxidant-rich blueberries and chia seeds, providing a great boost of energy and nutrients in a refreshing drink.

Servings: 2 | **Prep Time**: 5 minutes | **Cooking Time**: None

Ingredients:

- 1 cup blueberries (fresh or frozen)
- 1 tbsp chia seeds
- 1 banana, sliced
- 1/2 cup plain Greek yogurt
- 1/2 cup almond milk (or any milk of choice)
- 1 tsp honey or maple syrup (optional)
- 1/2 cup ice cubes

Preparation Steps:
Combine the blueberries, chia seeds, banana, Greek yogurt, almond milk, and ice cubes in a blender. Blend until smooth, adding more almond milk if needed to adjust the thickness. Taste and add honey or maple syrup if desired for sweetness. Serve immediately in two glasses.

Nutritional Value (per serving):
Calories: 180 | Protein: 6g | Fat: 4g | Carbohydrates: 32g | Fiber: 7g | Vitamin C: 20% DV | Calcium: 15% DV | Iron: 8% DV

29. Orange-Carrot Ginger Juice

This vibrant juice is a refreshing blend of oranges, carrots, and ginger, offering a boost of vitamin C, antioxidants, and anti-inflammatory properties.

Servings: 2 | **Prep Time**: 10 minutes | **Cooking Time**: None

Ingredients:

- 3 large oranges, peeled
- 2 large carrots, peeled and chopped
- 1-inch piece of fresh ginger, peeled
- 1/2 cup water (optional, for thinning)

Preparation Steps:
Juice the oranges, carrots, and ginger using a juicer. If you don't have a juicer, blend the ingredients in a blender with 1/2 cup of water, then strain through a fine-mesh sieve or cheesecloth. Pour into two glasses and serve immediately for a refreshing and health-boosting drink.

Nutritional Value (per serving):
Calories: 120 | Protein: 2g | Fat: 0g | Carbohydrates: 30g | Fiber: 4g | Vitamin A: 200% DV | Vitamin C: 150% DV | Potassium: 10% DV

30. Protein-Packed Banana Oat Muffins

These moist banana oat muffins are rich in protein and fiber, making them a great grab-and-go breakfast option. They are naturally sweetened with bananas and perfect for meal prep.

Servings: 6 muffins | **Prep Time**: 10 minutes | **Cooking Time**: 20 minutes

Ingredients:

- 2 ripe bananas, mashed
- 1 cup rolled oats
- 2 large eggs
- 1/4 cup Greek yogurt
- 1 tsp vanilla extract
- 1 tsp baking powder
- 1/2 tsp cinnamon
- 1/4 cup almond butter or peanut butter

Preparation Steps:
Preheat the oven to 350°F (175°C) and grease a muffin tin. In a mixing bowl, mash the bananas, then stir in the rolled oats, eggs, Greek yogurt, vanilla extract, baking powder, cinnamon, and almond butter until fully combined. Divide the batter evenly among the muffin cups and bake for 18-20 minutes, or

until a toothpick inserted in the center comes out clean. Let the muffins cool in the pan for 5 minutes before transferring to a wire rack. Enjoy warm or store in an airtight container for up to 3 days.

Nutritional Value (per muffin):
Calories: 180 | Protein: 7g | Fat: 7g | Carbohydrates: 23g | Fiber: 4g | Vitamin A: 2% DV | Potassium: 10% DV | Calcium: 6% DV

Chapter 4: Nutritious and Delicious Main Courses

31. Black Bean & Sweet Potato Tacos

These flavorful tacos combine the heartiness of black beans and the natural sweetness of roasted sweet potatoes, topped with fresh avocado and a zesty lime crema for a satisfying meal.

Servings: 4 | **Prep Time**: 15 minutes | **Cooking Time**: 25 minutes

Ingredients:

- 2 medium sweet potatoes, peeled and cubed
- 1 can black beans (15 oz), drained and rinsed
- 1 tbsp olive oil
- 1 tsp cumin
- 1 tsp paprika
- 1/2 tsp chili powder
- Salt and pepper to taste
- 8 small corn tortillas
- 1 avocado, sliced
- 1/4 cup fresh cilantro, chopped
- Lime wedges for serving

Preparation Steps:

Preheat the oven to 400°F (200°C). Toss the sweet potato cubes with olive oil, cumin, paprika, chili powder, salt, and pepper. Spread them on a baking sheet and roast for 20-25 minutes, until tender and lightly browned. Warm the tortillas in a dry skillet or oven, then fill each tortilla with roasted sweet potatoes, black beans, avocado slices, and a sprinkle of fresh cilantro. Serve with lime wedges for an extra burst of flavor.

Nutritional Value (per serving):

Calories: 300 | Protein: 9g | Fat: 10g | Carbohydrates: 48g | Fiber: 12g | Vitamin A: 200% DV | Vitamin C: 20% DV | Iron: 15% DV

32. Lentil Shepherd's Pie with Cauliflower Mash

This plant-based take on shepherd's pie uses a savory lentil filling topped with creamy cauliflower mash, creating a satisfying and nutritious comfort dish.

Servings: 4 | **Prep Time**: 20 minutes | **Cooking Time**: 40 minutes

Ingredients:

- 1 cup green or brown lentils, rinsed
- 2 cups vegetable broth
- 1 onion, diced
- 2 carrots, diced
- 2 celery stalks, diced
- 1 tbsp tomato paste
- 1 tsp thyme
- 1 tbsp olive oil
- 1 large head of cauliflower, chopped
- 1/4 cup almond milk (or any milk of choice)
- 1 tbsp butter or olive oil
- Salt and pepper to taste

Preparation Steps:
Cook the lentils in vegetable broth for 20-25 minutes, until tender, then set aside. In a large skillet, heat olive oil over medium heat and sauté the onion, carrots, and celery for 5-7 minutes, until softened. Stir in the tomato paste and thyme, then add the cooked lentils and season with salt and pepper. While the filling cooks, steam the cauliflower until tender, then mash with almond milk and butter until smooth. Transfer the lentil mixture to a baking dish, spreading the cauliflower mash over the top. Bake at 375°F (190°C) for 15-20 minutes, until the top is lightly golden.

Nutritional Value (per serving):
Calories: 320 | Protein: 14g | Fat: 10g | Carbohydrates: 45g | Fiber: 12g | Vitamin A: 80% DV | Vitamin C: 100% DV | Iron: 20% DV

33. Herb-Crusted Cod with Quinoa and Asparagus

This light yet flavorful dish features herb-crusted cod served alongside fluffy quinoa and tender asparagus, making it a well-balanced and nutritious meal.

Servings: 4 | **Prep Time**: 10 minutes | **Cooking Time**: 25 minutes

Ingredients:

- 4 cod fillets (4-6 oz each)
- 1 tbsp olive oil
- 1/4 cup fresh parsley, chopped
- 1 tsp lemon zest
- 1 cup quinoa, rinsed
- 2 cups vegetable broth
- 1 bunch asparagus, trimmed
- Salt and pepper to taste

Preparation Steps:
Preheat the oven to 400°F (200°C). In a small bowl, combine the parsley, lemon zest, and a pinch of salt and pepper. Rub the cod fillets with olive oil, then press the herb mixture onto each fillet. Place the cod on a baking sheet and bake for 12-15 minutes, until the fish is flaky. While the cod is baking, cook the quinoa in vegetable broth according to package instructions. Steam or roast the asparagus for 8-10 minutes until tender. Serve the cod with quinoa and asparagus on the side.

Nutritional Value (per serving):
Calories: 330 | Protein: 28g | Fat: 8g | Carbohydrates: 35g | Fiber: 5g | Vitamin C: 30% DV | Iron: 15% DV | Calcium: 6% DV

34. Turkey Meatballs with Zucchini Noodles

These lean turkey meatballs are served over spiralized zucchini noodles, providing a low-carb, high-protein alternative to traditional pasta dishes.

Servings: 4 | **Prep Time**: 15 minutes | **Cooking Time**: 20 minutes

Ingredients:

- 1 lb ground turkey
- 1/4 cup breadcrumbs (or almond flour for gluten-free)
- 1 egg
- 1/4 cup Parmesan cheese, grated (optional)
- 1 tsp garlic powder
- 1 tsp Italian seasoning
- 2 tbsp olive oil
- 4 medium zucchinis, spiralized
- Salt and pepper to taste
- Marinara sauce for serving

Preparation Steps:
In a large bowl, combine the ground turkey, breadcrumbs, egg, Parmesan cheese, garlic powder, Italian seasoning, salt, and pepper. Form the mixture into small meatballs. Heat olive oil in a large skillet over medium heat and cook the meatballs for 8-10 minutes, turning occasionally, until browned and cooked through. In a separate pan, sauté the zucchini noodles in olive oil for 2-3 minutes until just tender. Serve the meatballs over the zucchini noodles, topped with marinara sauce.

Nutritional Value (per serving):
Calories: 320 | Protein: 25g | Fat: 18g | Carbohydrates: 12g | Fiber: 4g | Vitamin A: 10% DV | Vitamin C: 35% DV | Iron: 15% DV

35. Spicy Chickpea & Quinoa Stew

This hearty, plant-based stew is packed with protein-rich chickpeas, quinoa, and flavorful spices, making it a perfect one-pot meal for any time of year.

Servings: 4 | **Prep Time**: 10 minutes | **Cooking Time**: 30 minutes

Ingredients:

- 1 cup quinoa, rinsed
- 1 can chickpeas (15 oz), drained and rinsed
- 1 onion, diced
- 2 cloves garlic, minced
- 1 tsp cumin
- 1 tsp smoked paprika

- 1/2 tsp cayenne pepper (optional)
- 1 can diced tomatoes (14 oz)
- 4 cups vegetable broth
- 2 tbsp olive oil
- Salt and pepper to taste
- Fresh cilantro for garnish

Preparation Steps:
In a large pot, heat olive oil over medium heat. Sauté the onion and garlic for 5 minutes until softened. Stir in the cumin, smoked paprika, and cayenne pepper, cooking for another minute. Add the quinoa, chickpeas, diced tomatoes, and vegetable broth. Bring to a boil, then reduce heat and simmer for 20-25 minutes, or until the quinoa is cooked and the stew has thickened. Season with salt and pepper to taste, and garnish with fresh cilantro before serving.

Nutritional Value (per serving):
Calories: 300 | Protein: 12g | Fat: 10g | Carbohydrates: 45g | Fiber: 10g | Vitamin C: 25% DV | Iron: 20% DV | Calcium: 8% DV

36. Grilled Shrimp with Garlic and Lemon Zest

These grilled shrimp are seasoned with garlic and lemon zest, providing a quick, flavorful meal that's perfect for light lunches or dinners.

Servings: 4 | **Prep Time**: 10 minutes | **Cooking Time**: 10 minutes

Ingredients:

- 1 lb shrimp, peeled and deveined
- 2 tbsp olive oil
- 3 cloves garlic, minced
- 1 tsp lemon zest
- 1 tbsp fresh lemon juice
- Salt and pepper to taste
- Fresh parsley for garnish

Preparation Steps:
In a bowl, toss the shrimp with olive oil, garlic, lemon zest, lemon juice, salt, and pepper. Preheat a grill or grill pan over medium-high heat. Grill the shrimp for

2-3 minutes on each side, until pink and cooked through. Serve hot, garnished with fresh parsley.

Nutritional Value (per serving):
Calories: 200 | Protein: 24g | Fat: 10g | Carbohydrates: 2g | Fiber: 0g | Vitamin C: 20% DV | Iron: 15% DV | Calcium: 10% DV

37. Roasted Eggplant & Hummus Wraps

These roasted eggplant wraps are paired with creamy hummus and fresh vegetables, making them a flavorful and filling plant-based meal.

Servings: 4 | **Prep Time**: 10 minutes | **Cooking Time**: 25 minutes

Ingredients:

- 1 large eggplant, sliced
- 2 tbsp olive oil
- Salt and pepper to taste
- 4 large whole wheat wraps
- 1/2 cup hummus
- 1 cup arugula
- 1/4 cup red onion, thinly sliced
- 1/4 cup fresh parsley, chopped

Preparation Steps:
Preheat the oven to 400°F (200°C). Toss the eggplant slices with olive oil, salt, and pepper, then spread them on a baking sheet. Roast for 20-25 minutes, until tender and golden brown. Warm the whole wheat wraps, then spread each with a generous layer of hummus. Top with roasted eggplant slices, arugula, red onion, and fresh parsley. Roll up the wraps and serve immediately.

Nutritional Value (per serving):
Calories: 290 | Protein: 8g | Fat: 14g | Carbohydrates: 35g | Fiber: 8g | Vitamin C: 15% DV | Iron: 10% DV | Calcium: 6% DV

38. One-Pot Chicken & Vegetable Stew

This comforting one-pot chicken and vegetable stew is packed with hearty ingredients like carrots, potatoes, and green beans, providing a warm and nutritious meal for cooler days.

Servings: 4 | **Prep Time**: 10 minutes | **Cooking Time**: 35 minutes

Ingredients:

- 4 boneless, skinless chicken thighs
- 1 onion, diced
- 2 carrots, sliced
- 2 potatoes, diced
- 1 cup green beans, trimmed
- 4 cups chicken broth
- 1 tbsp olive oil
- 1 tsp thyme
- Salt and pepper to taste

Preparation Steps:
In a large pot, heat olive oil over medium heat. Brown the chicken thighs for 3-4 minutes on each side, then remove from the pot and set aside. In the same pot, sauté the onion, carrots, and potatoes for 5 minutes until softened. Add the thyme, chicken broth, and browned chicken back into the pot. Bring to a boil, then reduce heat and simmer for 25 minutes, until the vegetables are tender and the chicken is cooked through. Stir in the green beans during the last 5 minutes of cooking. Season with salt and pepper to taste before serving.

Nutritional Value (per serving):
Calories: 380 | Protein: 30g | Fat: 15g | Carbohydrates: 30g | Fiber: 5g | Vitamin A: 80% DV | Iron: 15% DV | Calcium: 6% DV

39. Tofu Stir-Fry with Peanut Sauce

This quick and delicious stir-fry features tofu and vegetables tossed in a creamy peanut sauce, making it a satisfying plant-based meal.

Servings: 4 | **Prep Time**: 10 minutes | **Cooking Time**: 15 minutes

Ingredients:

- 1 block firm tofu, cubed
- 1 tbsp soy sauce
- 1 tbsp cornstarch
- 1 tbsp olive oil
- 1 bell pepper, sliced
- 1 zucchini, sliced
- 1/4 cup peanut butter
- 2 tbsp soy sauce
- 1 tbsp rice vinegar
- 1 tsp sesame oil
- 1 tsp honey
- 1/4 cup water

Preparation Steps:
Toss the tofu cubes in soy sauce and cornstarch. Heat olive oil in a skillet over medium heat and fry the tofu for 4-5 minutes until golden. Remove the tofu from the skillet and set aside. In the same skillet, stir-fry the bell pepper and zucchini for 5 minutes until tender. In a small bowl, whisk together the peanut butter, soy sauce, rice vinegar, sesame oil, honey, and water. Pour the sauce over the vegetables and stir to combine. Add the tofu back into the skillet and toss everything together. Serve warm.

Nutritional Value (per serving):
Calories: 320 | Protein: 15g | Fat: 20g | Carbohydrates: 18g | Fiber: 5g | Vitamin C: 50% DV | Iron: 15% DV | Calcium: 10% DV

40. Mediterranean Chicken Salad with Feta

This refreshing Mediterranean-inspired salad combines grilled chicken, fresh vegetables, and tangy feta cheese, all tossed in a light lemon-olive oil dressing.

Servings: 4 | **Prep Time**: 15 minutes | **Cooking Time**: 10 minutes

Ingredients:

- 2 boneless, skinless chicken breasts
- 1 tbsp olive oil

- 1 tsp oregano
- Salt and pepper to taste
- 4 cups mixed greens
- 1 cucumber, sliced
- 1/2 cup cherry tomatoes, halved
- 1/4 cup red onion, sliced
- 1/4 cup feta cheese, crumbled
- 2 tbsp lemon juice
- 2 tbsp olive oil

Preparation Steps:
Season the chicken breasts with olive oil, oregano, salt, and pepper. Grill the chicken for 5-6 minutes on each side, until cooked through. Let the chicken rest, then slice. In a large bowl, combine the mixed greens, cucumber, cherry tomatoes, red onion, and feta cheese. Whisk together the lemon juice and olive oil for the dressing, then toss with the salad. Top with sliced grilled chicken and serve.

Nutritional Value (per serving):
Calories: 280 | Protein: 26g | Fat: 16g | Carbohydrates: 10g | Fiber: 4g | Vitamin C: 20% DV | Calcium: 12% DV | Iron: 8% DV

Chapter 5: Plant-Based Power Meals

41. Quinoa & Roasted Veggie Bowl

This nutrient-dense bowl features fluffy quinoa and an array of roasted vegetables, making it a hearty and wholesome meal packed with fiber, vitamins, and minerals.

Servings: 4 | **Prep Time**: 10 minutes | **Cooking Time**: 30 minutes

Ingredients:

- 1 cup quinoa, rinsed
- 2 cups vegetable broth
- 1 zucchini, sliced
- 1 red bell pepper, diced
- 1 carrot, sliced
- 1 red onion, quartered
- 2 tbsp olive oil
- Salt and pepper to taste
- 1/4 cup fresh parsley, chopped

Preparation Steps:
Preheat the oven to 400°F (200°C). Toss the zucchini, bell pepper, carrot, and onion with olive oil, salt, and pepper. Spread them on a baking sheet and roast for 25-30 minutes, until tender and lightly browned. While the vegetables roast, bring the vegetable broth to a boil in a saucepan. Stir in the quinoa, reduce heat, cover, and simmer for 15 minutes or until the quinoa is cooked. Once the vegetables are done, combine them with the cooked quinoa and garnish with fresh parsley. Serve warm.

Nutritional Value (per serving):
Calories: 280 | Protein: 8g | Fat: 12g | Carbohydrates: 36g | Fiber: 6g | Vitamin A: 60% DV | Vitamin C: 40% DV | Iron: 10% DV

42. Sweet Potato & Black Bean Enchiladas

These flavorful enchiladas are filled with spiced sweet potatoes and black beans, then baked in a rich tomato sauce. They are a satisfying plant-based meal packed with fiber and protein.

Servings: 4 | **Prep Time**: 20 minutes | **Cooking Time**: 25 minutes

Ingredients:

- 2 medium sweet potatoes, peeled and cubed
- 1 can black beans (15 oz), drained and rinsed
- 8 small corn tortillas
- 1 can enchilada sauce (14 oz)
- 1 tsp cumin
- 1 tsp paprika
- 1/2 tsp chili powder
- 1 tbsp olive oil
- 1/4 cup fresh cilantro, chopped
- Salt and pepper to taste

Preparation Steps:
Preheat the oven to 375°F (190°C). In a large skillet, heat the olive oil over medium heat. Add the sweet potatoes, cumin, paprika, chili powder, salt, and pepper, and cook for 8-10 minutes, until the sweet potatoes are tender. Stir in the black beans and cook for another 2 minutes. Fill each tortilla with the sweet potato and black bean mixture, roll up, and place seam-side down in a baking dish. Pour the enchilada sauce over the top and bake for 20-25 minutes, until heated through. Garnish with fresh cilantro and serve.

Nutritional Value (per serving):
Calories: 320 | Protein: 10g | Fat: 8g | Carbohydrates: 56g | Fiber: 12g | Vitamin A: 180% DV | Vitamin C: 20% DV | Iron: 15% DV

43. Tofu & Vegetable Stir-Fry

This quick and easy stir-fry features tofu and a medley of colorful vegetables tossed in a flavorful soy-ginger sauce. It's a healthy and satisfying meal full of protein and nutrients.

Servings: 4 | **Prep Time**: 10 minutes | **Cooking Time**: 15 minutes

Ingredients:

- 1 block firm tofu, cubed
- 1 tbsp cornstarch
- 2 tbsp soy sauce
- 1 tbsp sesame oil
- 1 bell pepper, sliced
- 1 zucchini, sliced
- 1 carrot, julienned
- 1 tbsp fresh ginger, minced
- 2 tbsp soy sauce
- 1 tbsp rice vinegar
- 1 tsp honey or maple syrup
- 1 tbsp sesame seeds for garnish (optional)

Preparation Steps:
Toss the tofu cubes in soy sauce and cornstarch. Heat sesame oil in a large skillet or wok over medium-high heat and cook the tofu for 5-7 minutes, turning occasionally, until golden and crispy. Remove the tofu and set aside. In the same skillet, stir-fry the bell pepper, zucchini, and carrot for 5 minutes until tender. Add the ginger, soy sauce, rice vinegar, and honey, and toss to combine. Return the tofu to the skillet and stir everything together. Garnish with sesame seeds and serve hot.

Nutritional Value (per serving):
Calories: 280 | Protein: 14g | Fat: 12g | Carbohydrates: 26g | Fiber: 5g | Vitamin A: 80% DV | Iron: 15% DV | Calcium: 10% DV

44. Roasted Cauliflower Tacos

These flavorful tacos feature roasted spiced cauliflower and fresh toppings, providing a delicious and healthy plant-based option for taco night.

Servings: 4 | **Prep Time**: 10 minutes | **Cooking Time**: 25 minutes

Ingredients:

- 1 large head cauliflower, cut into florets
- 2 tbsp olive oil
- 1 tsp smoked paprika
- 1/2 tsp cumin
- 1/2 tsp chili powder
- Salt and pepper to taste
- 8 small corn tortillas
- 1 avocado, sliced
- 1/4 cup fresh cilantro, chopped
- Lime wedges for serving

Preparation Steps:
Preheat the oven to 400°F (200°C). Toss the cauliflower florets with olive oil, smoked paprika, cumin, chili powder, salt, and pepper. Spread them on a baking sheet and roast for 20-25 minutes, until tender and slightly crispy. Warm the tortillas, then fill each with roasted cauliflower, avocado slices, and a sprinkle of fresh cilantro. Serve with lime wedges for extra flavor.

Nutritional Value (per serving):
Calories: 270 | Protein: 6g | Fat: 15g | Carbohydrates: 32g | Fiber: 8g | Vitamin A: 10% DV | Vitamin C: 70% DV | Iron: 10% DV

45. Zucchini Noodles with Pesto

This light and refreshing dish features spiralized zucchini noodles tossed in a vibrant homemade basil pesto, making it a perfect low-carb, nutrient-packed meal.

Servings: 4 | **Prep Time**: 10 minutes | **Cooking Time**: None

Ingredients:

- 4 medium zucchinis, spiralized
- 1 cup fresh basil leaves
- 1/4 cup pine nuts or walnuts
- 1/4 cup Parmesan cheese (optional)
- 1 clove garlic
- 1/4 cup olive oil
- Salt and pepper to taste

- Cherry tomatoes for garnish (optional)

Preparation Steps:
In a food processor, combine the basil, pine nuts, Parmesan cheese (if using), garlic, olive oil, salt, and pepper. Blend until smooth, adding more olive oil if needed to reach your desired consistency. Toss the spiralized zucchini noodles with the pesto until evenly coated. Garnish with cherry tomatoes and serve immediately.

Nutritional Value (per serving):
Calories: 240 | Protein: 6g | Fat: 20g | Carbohydrates: 10g | Fiber: 4g | Vitamin A: 25% DV | Vitamin C: 40% DV | Iron: 8% DV

46. Lentil Salad with Lemon Vinaigrette

This refreshing lentil salad is full of protein and fiber, tossed with a tangy lemon vinaigrette for a bright and flavorful plant-based dish.

Servings: 4 | **Prep Time**: 10 minutes | **Cooking Time**: 20 minutes

Ingredients:

- 1 cup green lentils, rinsed
- 2 cups vegetable broth
- 1 cucumber, diced
- 1/2 red onion, diced
- 1/4 cup fresh parsley, chopped
- 1/4 cup olive oil
- 2 tbsp lemon juice
- 1 tsp Dijon mustard
- Salt and pepper to taste

Preparation Steps:
Cook the lentils in vegetable broth for 20 minutes, or until tender. Drain and let cool slightly. In a large bowl, combine the cooked lentils, cucumber, red onion, and parsley. In a small bowl, whisk together the olive oil, lemon juice, Dijon mustard, salt, and pepper. Pour the vinaigrette over the salad and toss to combine. Serve chilled or at room temperature.

Nutritional Value (per serving):
Calories: 260 | Protein: 10g | Fat: 14g | Carbohydrates: 26g | Fiber: 10g | Vitamin C: 15% DV | Iron: 20% DV | Calcium: 6% DV

47. Spinach and Chickpea Curry

This warm and comforting spinach and chickpea curry is rich in flavor and packed with plant-based protein, making it a hearty and satisfying meal.

Servings: 4 | **Prep Time**: 10 minutes | **Cooking Time**: 20 minutes

Ingredients:

- 1 tbsp olive oil
- 1 onion, diced
- 3 cloves garlic, minced
- 1 tbsp curry powder
- 1/2 tsp turmeric
- 1 can chickpeas (15 oz), drained and rinsed
- 1 can diced tomatoes (14 oz)
- 4 cups fresh spinach
- 1/2 cup coconut milk
- Salt and pepper to taste

Preparation Steps:
Heat olive oil in a large skillet over medium heat. Add the onion and garlic, cooking until softened, about 5 minutes. Stir in the curry powder and turmeric, and cook for 1 minute. Add the chickpeas and diced tomatoes, and simmer for 10 minutes. Stir in the spinach and coconut milk, cooking until the spinach wilts. Season with salt and pepper to taste and serve warm.

Nutritional Value (per serving):
Calories: 300 | Protein: 9g | Fat: 14g | Carbohydrates: 36g | Fiber: 10g | Vitamin A: 70% DV | Vitamin C: 25% DV | Iron: 20% DV

48. Grilled Portobello Mushrooms with Balsamic Glaze

These hearty grilled portobello mushrooms are marinated in a flavorful balsamic glaze, making them a delicious and satisfying plant-based entrée or side dish.

Servings: 4 | **Prep Time**: 10 minutes | **Cooking Time**: 10 minutes

Ingredients:

- 4 large portobello mushrooms
- 2 tbsp balsamic vinegar
- 2 tbsp olive oil
- 1 tsp garlic powder
- Salt and pepper to taste
- Fresh parsley for garnish

Preparation Steps:
In a small bowl, whisk together the balsamic vinegar, olive oil, garlic powder, salt, and pepper. Brush the mushrooms generously with the marinade and let them sit for 10 minutes. Preheat a grill or grill pan over medium-high heat. Grill the mushrooms for 5 minutes on each side, or until tender. Garnish with fresh parsley and serve.

Nutritional Value (per serving):
Calories: 130 | Protein: 3g | Fat: 10g | Carbohydrates: 8g | Fiber: 2g | Vitamin D: 40% DV | Iron: 6% DV | Potassium: 15% DV

49. Vegan Stuffed Peppers

These colorful bell peppers are stuffed with a hearty mixture of rice, black beans, and vegetables, creating a flavorful and filling plant-based meal.

Servings: 4 | **Prep Time**: 15 minutes | **Cooking Time**: 30 minutes

Ingredients:

- 4 large bell peppers, tops cut off and seeds removed
- 1 cup cooked brown rice
- 1 can black beans (15 oz), drained and rinsed
- 1/2 cup corn kernels
- 1/2 cup diced tomatoes
- 1 tsp cumin
- 1 tsp paprika
- Salt and pepper to taste

- Fresh cilantro for garnish

Preparation Steps:
Preheat the oven to 375°F (190°C). In a large bowl, combine the cooked brown rice, black beans, corn, diced tomatoes, cumin, paprika, salt, and pepper. Stuff the bell peppers with the rice mixture and place them in a baking dish. Bake for 25-30 minutes, until the peppers are tender. Garnish with fresh cilantro and serve.

Nutritional Value (per serving):
Calories: 280 | Protein: 10g | Fat: 6g | Carbohydrates: 48g | Fiber: 12g | Vitamin A: 60% DV | Vitamin C: 120% DV | Iron: 15% DV

50. Roasted Beet and Arugula Salad

This refreshing salad features earthy roasted beets and peppery arugula, tossed with a simple balsamic vinaigrette for a light and nutritious meal.

Servings: 4 | **Prep Time**: 10 minutes | **Cooking Time**: 40 minutes

Ingredients:

- 4 medium beets, peeled and cubed
- 2 tbsp olive oil
- 4 cups fresh arugula
- 1/4 cup walnuts, chopped
- 1/4 cup crumbled feta (optional)
- 2 tbsp balsamic vinegar
- Salt and pepper to taste

Preparation Steps:
Preheat the oven to 400°F (200°C). Toss the beets with olive oil, salt, and pepper, and spread them on a baking sheet. Roast for 35-40 minutes, until tender. In a large bowl, combine the roasted beets, arugula, walnuts, and feta if using. Drizzle with balsamic vinegar and toss to combine. Serve chilled or at room temperature.

Nutritional Value (per serving):
Calories: 240 | Protein: 5g | Fat: 14g | Carbohydrates: 24g | Fiber: 6g | Vitamin A: 15% DV | Vitamin C: 25% DV | Iron: 10% DV

Chapter 6: Healthy Snacks for Every Occasion

51. Roasted Almond & Cranberry Trail Mix

This simple, homemade trail mix combines roasted almonds and dried cranberries, providing a perfect balance of healthy fats, fiber, and natural sweetness for an on-the-go snack.

Servings: 4 | **Prep Time**: 5 minutes | **Cooking Time**: 10 minutes

Ingredients:

- 1 cup almonds
- 1/2 cup dried cranberries
- 1/4 cup pumpkin seeds
- 1 tbsp olive oil
- 1/2 tsp sea salt
- 1/4 tsp cinnamon (optional)

Preparation Steps:
Preheat the oven to 350°F (175°C). Toss the almonds with olive oil and spread them on a baking sheet. Roast for 8-10 minutes until golden and fragrant. Let the almonds cool, then mix with dried cranberries, pumpkin seeds, and a sprinkle of sea salt and cinnamon if desired. Store in an airtight container for up to a week.

Nutritional Value (per serving):
Calories: 220 | Protein: 6g | Fat: 15g | Carbohydrates: 18g | Fiber: 4g | Vitamin E: 25% DV | Iron: 8% DV | Calcium: 6% DV

52. Homemade Granola Bars with Oats and Dates

These chewy granola bars are packed with oats, dates, and nuts, offering a delicious and energy-boosting snack that's perfect for any time of day.

Servings: 8 bars | **Prep Time**: 10 minutes | **Cooking Time**: 20 minutes

Ingredients:

- 1 1/2 cups rolled oats
- 1/2 cup dates, pitted and chopped
- 1/4 cup honey or maple syrup
- 1/4 cup almond butter
- 1/4 cup chopped almonds
- 1/4 cup dried cranberries
- 1 tsp vanilla extract
- 1/4 tsp cinnamon

Preparation Steps:
Preheat the oven to 350°F (175°C) and line a baking dish with parchment paper. In a saucepan, warm the honey and almond butter until melted and smooth. In a large bowl, mix the oats, dates, almonds, cranberries, vanilla extract, and cinnamon. Pour the warm honey mixture over the oat mixture and stir until combined. Press the mixture into the prepared baking dish and bake for 15-20 minutes until set. Let cool before cutting into bars.

Nutritional Value (per bar):
Calories: 180 | Protein: 4g | Fat: 7g | Carbohydrates: 28g | Fiber: 3g | Vitamin E: 10% DV | Iron: 6% DV | Calcium: 6% DV

53. Fruit Salad with Mint and Lime

A refreshing and colorful mix of seasonal fruits, this fruit salad is enhanced with fresh mint and a zesty lime dressing for a light and nutritious snack.

Servings: 4 | **Prep Time**: 10 minutes | **Cooking Time**: None

Ingredients:

- 1 cup strawberries, hulled and sliced
- 1 cup blueberries
- 1 cup diced pineapple
- 1 kiwi, peeled and sliced
- 1 tbsp fresh lime juice
- 1 tbsp honey (optional)
- 2 tbsp fresh mint, chopped

Preparation Steps:
In a large bowl, combine the strawberries, blueberries, pineapple, and kiwi. Drizzle with fresh lime juice and honey if using. Sprinkle with chopped mint and toss gently to combine. Serve immediately for a refreshing snack or dessert.

Nutritional Value (per serving):
Calories: 90 | Protein: 1g | Fat: 0g | Carbohydrates: 22g | Fiber: 4g | Vitamin C: 120% DV | Iron: 2% DV | Calcium: 2% DV

54. Baked Apple Chips

These crunchy and naturally sweet baked apple chips are a healthy alternative to store-bought chips, making them the perfect snack for satisfying cravings.

Servings: 4 | **Prep Time**: 5 minutes | **Cooking Time**: 2 hours

Ingredients:

- 2 large apples, thinly sliced
- 1/2 tsp cinnamon
- 1 tbsp honey (optional)

Preparation Steps:
Preheat the oven to 200°F (95°C). Arrange the apple slices in a single layer on a baking sheet lined with parchment paper. Sprinkle with cinnamon and drizzle with honey if using. Bake for 1.5-2 hours, flipping halfway through, until the apples are crisp. Let cool before serving or storing in an airtight container.

Nutritional Value (per serving):
Calories: 80 | Protein: 0g | Fat: 0g | Carbohydrates: 22g | Fiber: 4g | Vitamin C: 10% DV | Iron: 2% DV | Calcium: 2% DV

55. Cucumber & Hummus Bites

These refreshing cucumber bites are topped with creamy hummus, providing a low-calorie, nutrient-dense snack that's perfect for any occasion.

Servings: 4 | **Prep Time**: 5 minutes | **Cooking Time**: None

Ingredients:

- 1 large cucumber, sliced
- 1/2 cup hummus
- 1 tbsp olive oil
- 1/4 tsp paprika
- Fresh parsley for garnish

Preparation Steps:
Arrange the cucumber slices on a serving plate. Top each slice with a dollop of hummus, then drizzle with olive oil and sprinkle with paprika. Garnish with fresh parsley and serve immediately for a light, refreshing snack.

Nutritional Value (per serving):
Calories: 100 | Protein: 3g | Fat: 6g | Carbohydrates: 10g | Fiber: 3g | Vitamin A: 4% DV | Vitamin C: 6% DV | Iron: 4% DV

56. Chia Seed Pudding with Mango

This creamy chia seed pudding is naturally sweetened with fresh mango and makes for a delicious, nutrient-packed snack or breakfast.

Servings: 2 | **Prep Time**: 5 minutes | **Cooking Time**: None (overnight chill)

Ingredients:

- 1/4 cup chia seeds
- 1 cup almond milk (or any milk of choice)
- 1 tsp vanilla extract
- 1 tbsp honey or maple syrup (optional)
- 1/2 cup diced mango

Preparation Steps:
In a small bowl or jar, whisk together the chia seeds, almond milk, vanilla extract, and honey or maple syrup if using. Cover and refrigerate overnight or for at least 4 hours, until the mixture thickens into a pudding. When ready to serve, top the chia pudding with fresh diced mango and enjoy.

Nutritional Value (per serving):
Calories: 180 | Protein: 5g | Fat: 8g | Carbohydrates: 25g | Fiber: 9g | Vitamin C: 40% DV | Iron: 10% DV | Calcium: 15% DV

57. Veggie Sticks with Avocado Dip

This light and flavorful avocado dip is the perfect complement to crunchy veggie sticks, making it a nutrient-rich snack packed with healthy fats and fiber.

Servings: 4 | **Prep Time**: 10 minutes | **Cooking Time**: None

Ingredients:

- 1 ripe avocado, mashed
- 1 tbsp lime juice
- 1/4 cup plain Greek yogurt
- 1/4 tsp garlic powder
- Salt and pepper to taste
- Carrot sticks, cucumber sticks, and bell pepper strips for serving

Preparation Steps:
In a small bowl, mash the avocado and mix in the lime juice, Greek yogurt, garlic powder, salt, and pepper until smooth and creamy. Serve the avocado dip with assorted veggie sticks for a healthy, satisfying snack.

Nutritional Value (per serving):
Calories: 150 | Protein: 3g | Fat: 12g | Carbohydrates: 10g | Fiber: 5g | Vitamin A: 60% DV | Vitamin C: 70% DV | Iron: 6% DV

58. Energy Balls with Peanut Butter and Flaxseeds

These no-bake energy balls are loaded with peanut butter, oats, and flaxseeds, providing a convenient and nutritious snack that's great for on-the-go energy.

Servings: 12 balls | **Prep Time**: 10 minutes | **Cooking Time**: None

Ingredients:

- 1 cup rolled oats
- 1/2 cup peanut butter
- 1/4 cup honey or maple syrup

- 1/4 cup ground flaxseeds
- 1/4 cup mini dark chocolate chips (optional)
- 1 tsp vanilla extract

Preparation Steps:
In a large bowl, combine the oats, peanut butter, honey, ground flaxseeds, chocolate chips, and vanilla extract. Stir until fully combined. Roll the mixture into 12 small balls and place them on a baking sheet. Refrigerate for 30 minutes to set. Store the energy balls in an airtight container in the fridge for up to a week.

Nutritional Value (per ball):
Calories: 100 | Protein: 3g | Fat: 6g | Carbohydrates: 10g | Fiber: 2g | Vitamin E: 4% DV | Iron: 4% DV | Calcium: 2% DV

59. Dark Chocolate Almond Bark

This indulgent yet healthy treat combines rich dark chocolate with crunchy almonds, providing a satisfying snack that's full of antioxidants and healthy fats.

Servings: 8 | **Prep Time**: 10 minutes | **Cooking Time**: 10 minutes

Ingredients:

- 1 cup dark chocolate chips
- 1/2 cup almonds, chopped
- 1/4 tsp sea salt

Preparation Steps:
Melt the dark chocolate chips in a microwave or over a double boiler. Stir in the chopped almonds and spread the mixture onto a baking sheet lined with parchment paper. Sprinkle with sea salt and refrigerate for 20 minutes or until set. Break the chocolate bark into pieces and store in an airtight container.

Nutritional Value (per serving):
Calories: 170 | Protein: 3g | Fat: 12g | Carbohydrates: 14g | Fiber: 3g | Iron: 10% DV | Calcium: 2% DV

60. Greek Yogurt with Honey and Berries

This quick and easy snack combines creamy Greek yogurt with fresh berries and a drizzle of honey, offering a perfect balance of protein and natural sweetness.

Servings: 2 | **Prep Time**: 5 minutes | **Cooking Time**: None

Ingredients:

- 1 cup plain Greek yogurt
- 1/2 cup mixed berries (blueberries, strawberries, raspberries)
- 1 tbsp honey
- 1 tbsp chia seeds (optional)

Preparation Steps:
Divide the Greek yogurt between two bowls. Top with mixed berries and drizzle with honey. Sprinkle with chia seeds if desired for an added nutrient boost. Serve immediately for a refreshing and satisfying snack.

Nutritional Value (per serving):
Calories: 160 | Protein: 10g | Fat: 3g | Carbohydrates: 25g | Fiber: 4g | Vitamin C: 20% DV | Calcium: 15% DV | Iron: 4% DV

Chapter 7: Smoothies and Juices for Energy Boosts

61. Spinach & Pineapple Smoothie

This refreshing smoothie blends spinach with sweet pineapple, creating a nutrient-rich, energizing drink that's perfect for any time of day.

Servings: 2 | **Prep Time**: 5 minutes | **Cooking Time**: None

Ingredients:

- 1 cup fresh spinach
- 1/2 cup pineapple chunks (fresh or frozen)
- 1 banana
- 1/2 cup coconut water or almond milk
- 1 tbsp chia seeds (optional)
- Ice cubes

Preparation Steps:
Combine the spinach, pineapple, banana, and coconut water in a blender. Add ice cubes and chia seeds if using, then blend until smooth. Serve immediately for a refreshing and energizing boost.

Nutritional Value (per serving):
Calories: 120 | Protein: 2g | Fat: 1g | Carbohydrates: 30g | Fiber: 5g | Vitamin A: 40% DV | Vitamin C: 80% DV | Iron: 6% DV

62. Berry & Almond Milk Smoothie

A creamy and antioxidant-packed smoothie, this blend of mixed berries and almond milk provides a delicious and nutritious way to start your day.

Servings: 2 | **Prep Time**: 5 minutes | **Cooking Time**: None

Ingredients:

- 1 cup mixed berries (blueberries, strawberries, raspberries)
- 1 banana
- 1 cup almond milk
- 1 tsp honey or maple syrup (optional)
- Ice cubes

Preparation Steps:
In a blender, combine the mixed berries, banana, almond milk, and ice cubes. Blend until smooth, adding honey if you prefer a sweeter smoothie. Serve chilled.

Nutritional Value (per serving):
Calories: 150 | Protein: 2g | Fat: 3g | Carbohydrates: 30g | Fiber: 6g | Vitamin C: 50% DV | Calcium: 20% DV | Iron: 4% DV

63. Green Detox Juice with Cucumber and Apple

This revitalizing green juice is made with hydrating cucumber, sweet apple, and a hint of lemon, making it a perfect detoxifying drink.

Servings: 2 | **Prep Time**: 10 minutes | **Cooking Time**: None

Ingredients:

- 1 cucumber
- 1 apple
- 1/2 lemon, juiced
- 1 handful fresh spinach
- 1/2 cup water or coconut water

Preparation Steps:
In a blender or juicer, combine the cucumber, apple, lemon juice, spinach, and water. Blend until smooth, then strain through a fine-mesh sieve if you prefer a thinner juice. Serve immediately for a hydrating, detoxifying drink.

Nutritional Value (per serving):
Calories: 70 | Protein: 1g | Fat: 0g | Carbohydrates: 18g | Fiber: 3g | Vitamin C: 25% DV | Calcium: 4% DV | Iron: 6% DV

64. Carrot & Ginger Juice

This vibrant juice combines sweet carrots with spicy ginger, creating a refreshing and immune-boosting drink rich in vitamins A and C.

Servings: 2 | **Prep Time**: 10 minutes | **Cooking Time**: None

Ingredients:

- 4 large carrots, peeled
- 1-inch piece fresh ginger, peeled
- 1/2 lemon, juiced
- 1/2 cup water

Preparation Steps:
Juice the carrots and ginger using a juicer, or blend them in a high-speed blender with the water and lemon juice. Strain the mixture through a fine-mesh sieve if desired. Serve immediately and enjoy the refreshing zing.

Nutritional Value (per serving):
Calories: 60 | Protein: 1g | Fat: 0g | Carbohydrates: 14g | Fiber: 3g | Vitamin A: 350% DV | Vitamin C: 20% DV | Iron: 4% DV

65. Watermelon & Mint Smoothie

This hydrating and refreshing smoothie combines sweet watermelon with cool mint for a perfect summer drink.

Servings: 2 | **Prep Time**: 5 minutes | **Cooking Time**: None

Ingredients:

- 2 cups watermelon, cubed
- 1/2 cup coconut water
- 1 tbsp fresh mint leaves
- Juice of 1/2 lime
- Ice cubes

Preparation Steps:
In a blender, combine the watermelon, coconut water, mint, and lime juice. Add ice cubes and blend until smooth. Serve chilled for a hydrating treat.

Nutritional Value (per serving):
Calories: 60 | Protein: 1g | Fat: 0g | Carbohydrates: 15g | Fiber: 1g | Vitamin C: 15% DV | Calcium: 2% DV | Iron: 2% DV

66. Turmeric & Coconut Smoothie

This anti-inflammatory smoothie is made with turmeric, coconut milk, and a hint of ginger, providing a creamy, nourishing drink to start your day.

Servings: 2 | **Prep Time**: 5 minutes | **Cooking Time**: None

Ingredients:

- 1 cup coconut milk
- 1 banana
- 1 tsp ground turmeric
- 1/2 tsp fresh ginger, grated
- 1 tsp honey or maple syrup (optional)
- Ice cubes

Preparation Steps:
Blend the coconut milk, banana, turmeric, ginger, and honey until smooth. Add ice cubes and blend again until creamy. Serve immediately.

Nutritional Value (per serving):
Calories: 150 | Protein: 2g | Fat: 10g | Carbohydrates: 18g | Fiber: 2g | Vitamin C: 6% DV | Calcium: 4% DV | Iron: 6% DV

67. Banana & Peanut Butter Protein Smoothie

This creamy smoothie blends banana with peanut butter and plant-based protein powder for a delicious and filling post-workout drink.

Servings: 2 | **Prep Time**: 5 minutes | **Cooking Time**: None

Ingredients:

- 1 banana
- 2 tbsp peanut butter
- 1 scoop plant-based protein powder
- 1 cup almond milk
- Ice cubes

Preparation Steps:
Blend the banana, peanut butter, protein powder, and almond milk until smooth. Add ice cubes and blend until creamy. Serve immediately for a protein-packed boost.

Nutritional Value (per serving):
Calories: 250 | Protein: 15g | Fat: 12g | Carbohydrates: 25g | Fiber: 4g | Vitamin E: 10% DV | Calcium: 20% DV | Iron: 10% DV

68. Raspberry & Chia Seed Smoothie

This antioxidant-rich smoothie combines tart raspberries with chia seeds, creating a refreshing and nutrient-dense drink.

Servings: 2 | **Prep Time**: 5 minutes | **Cooking Time**: None

Ingredients:

- 1 cup raspberries (fresh or frozen)
- 1 banana
- 1 tbsp chia seeds
- 1 cup almond milk
- 1 tsp honey or maple syrup (optional)

Preparation Steps:
Blend the raspberries, banana, chia seeds, almond milk, and honey until smooth. Serve immediately for a refreshing, antioxidant-rich drink.

Nutritional Value (per serving):
Calories: 180 | Protein: 4g | Fat: 5g | Carbohydrates: 30g | Fiber: 10g | Vitamin C: 40% DV | Calcium: 15% DV | Iron: 8% DV

69. Avocado & Coconut Milk Smoothie

This rich and creamy smoothie blends avocado and coconut milk for a velvety drink that's packed with healthy fats and fiber.

Servings: 2 | **Prep Time**: 5 minutes | **Cooking Time**: None

Ingredients:

- 1 ripe avocado
- 1 cup coconut milk
- 1 banana
- 1 tsp vanilla extract
- 1 tsp honey or maple syrup (optional)

Preparation Steps:
Blend the avocado, coconut milk, banana, vanilla extract, and honey until smooth. Serve chilled for a nourishing, creamy treat.

Nutritional Value (per serving):
Calories: 220 | Protein: 2g | Fat: 18g | Carbohydrates: 20g | Fiber: 6g | Vitamin E: 10% DV | Calcium: 4% DV | Iron: 6% DV

70. Tropical Fruit Juice with Mango and Passion Fruit

This tropical juice combines mango and passion fruit for a sweet and tangy drink that's bursting with vitamins and antioxidants.

Servings: 2 | **Prep Time**: 5 minutes | **Cooking Time**: None

Ingredients:

- 1 ripe mango, peeled and diced
- 1 passion fruit, pulp scooped out
- 1/2 cup pineapple juice
- 1/2 cup coconut water
- Ice cubes

Preparation Steps:
Blend the mango, passion fruit pulp, pineapple juice, and coconut water until smooth. Serve chilled over ice for a tropical refreshment.

Nutritional Value (per serving):
Calories: 120 | Protein: 1g | Fat: 0g | Carbohydrates: 30g | Fiber: 3g | Vitamin C: 80% DV | Iron: 4% DV | Potassium: 8% DV

Chapter 8: Delicious Desserts Without Guilt

71. Baked Apples with Cinnamon & Walnuts

These warm baked apples are spiced with cinnamon and stuffed with walnuts, providing a naturally sweet and comforting dessert that's perfect for fall.

Servings: 4 | **Prep Time**: 10 minutes | **Cooking Time**: 30 minutes

Ingredients:

- 4 medium apples, cored
- 1/4 cup chopped walnuts
- 1 tbsp honey or maple syrup
- 1 tsp ground cinnamon
- 1/4 tsp nutmeg

Preparation Steps:
Preheat the oven to 350°F (175°C). In a small bowl, mix the chopped walnuts, honey, cinnamon, and nutmeg. Stuff the apples with the walnut mixture, then place them in a baking dish. Add a few tablespoons of water to the bottom of the dish to prevent sticking. Bake for 25-30 minutes, until the apples are tender. Serve warm.

Nutritional Value (per serving):
Calories: 180 | Protein: 2g | Fat: 6g | Carbohydrates: 32g | Fiber: 6g | Vitamin C: 15% DV | Calcium: 4% DV | Iron: 4% DV

72. Dark Chocolate Avocado Mousse

This rich and creamy avocado mousse is made with dark chocolate and naturally sweetened with honey, offering a decadent yet healthy dessert.

Servings: 4 | **Prep Time**: 10 minutes | **Cooking Time**: None

Ingredients:

- 2 ripe avocados
- 1/4 cup unsweetened cocoa powder
- 1/4 cup dark chocolate chips, melted
- 2 tbsp honey or maple syrup
- 1 tsp vanilla extract

Preparation Steps:
In a blender or food processor, combine the avocados, cocoa powder, melted dark chocolate, honey, and vanilla extract. Blend until smooth and creamy. Chill in the refrigerator for 30 minutes before serving. Garnish with fresh berries or shaved chocolate if desired.

Nutritional Value (per serving):
Calories: 200 | Protein: 3g | Fat: 16g | Carbohydrates: 18g | Fiber: 6g | Vitamin E: 10% DV | Iron: 15% DV | Calcium: 4% DV

73. Honey-Sweetened Greek Yogurt Parfait

This light and refreshing parfait combines protein-rich Greek yogurt with honey, fresh fruits, and a crunchy topping of granola or nuts.

Servings: 2 | **Prep Time**: 5 minutes | **Cooking Time**: None

Ingredients:

- 1 cup plain Greek yogurt
- 2 tbsp honey
- 1/2 cup mixed berries (blueberries, strawberries, raspberries)
- 1/4 cup granola or chopped nuts

Preparation Steps:
In two serving bowls or glasses, layer half of the Greek yogurt, drizzle with honey, and top with mixed berries. Repeat the layers, then sprinkle granola or chopped nuts on top for added crunch. Serve immediately.

Nutritional Value (per serving):
Calories: 220 | Protein: 12g | Fat: 5g | Carbohydrates: 30g | Fiber: 3g | Vitamin C: 20% DV | Calcium: 15% DV | Iron: 4% DV

74. Chia Seed Pudding with Berries

This creamy chia seed pudding is packed with fiber and omega-3s, topped with antioxidant-rich berries for a light and nutritious dessert.

Servings: 2 | **Prep Time**: 5 minutes | **Cooking Time**: None (chill overnight)

Ingredients:

- 1/4 cup chia seeds
- 1 cup almond milk (or any milk of choice)
- 1 tsp vanilla extract
- 1 tbsp honey or maple syrup
- 1/2 cup mixed berries

Preparation Steps:
In a bowl or jar, whisk together the chia seeds, almond milk, vanilla extract, and honey. Cover and refrigerate for at least 4 hours or overnight, until the mixture thickens. When ready to serve, top the chia pudding with fresh berries and enjoy.

Nutritional Value (per serving):
Calories: 180 | Protein: 4g | Fat: 8g | Carbohydrates: 25g | Fiber: 10g | Vitamin C: 20% DV | Calcium: 15% DV | Iron: 10% DV

75. Coconut & Almond Bliss Balls

These no-bake bliss balls are a combination of coconut, almonds, and dates, creating a naturally sweet and wholesome snack or dessert.

Servings: 12 balls | **Prep Time**: 10 minutes | **Cooking Time**: None

Ingredients:

- 1 cup shredded coconut
- 1/2 cup almonds
- 1/2 cup dates, pitted
- 1 tbsp coconut oil
- 1 tsp vanilla extract

Preparation Steps:
In a food processor, blend the shredded coconut, almonds, dates, coconut oil, and vanilla extract until the mixture is well combined and sticks together. Roll the mixture into small balls and refrigerate for 30 minutes to set. Store in the fridge for up to a week.

Nutritional Value (per ball):
Calories: 90 | Protein: 2g | Fat: 6g | Carbohydrates: 10g | Fiber: 2g | Vitamin E: 4% DV | Iron: 4% DV | Calcium: 2% DV

76. Carrot Cake Energy Bites

These raw energy bites taste just like carrot cake but are made with wholesome ingredients like carrots, oats, and almonds for a nutritious treat.

Servings: 12 bites | **Prep Time**: 10 minutes | **Cooking Time**: None

Ingredients:

- 1 cup shredded carrots
- 1/2 cup rolled oats
- 1/4 cup almonds, chopped
- 1/4 cup raisins
- 2 tbsp honey or maple syrup
- 1 tsp cinnamon
- 1/2 tsp vanilla extract

Preparation Steps:
In a food processor, pulse together the shredded carrots, oats, almonds, raisins, honey, cinnamon, and vanilla extract until well combined. Roll the mixture into small bites and refrigerate for 30 minutes to set. Store in the fridge for up to a week.

Nutritional Value (per bite):
Calories: 80 | Protein: 2g | Fat: 3g | Carbohydrates: 12g | Fiber: 2g | Vitamin A: 50% DV | Iron: 4% DV | Calcium: 2% DV

77. Mango Sorbet with Lime

This refreshing mango sorbet is naturally sweetened with ripe mangoes and a splash of lime, making it a healthy and delicious frozen dessert.

Servings: 4 | **Prep Time**: 5 minutes | **Cooking Time**: None (freeze for 2 hours)

Ingredients:

- 2 ripe mangoes, peeled and diced
- Juice of 1 lime
- 1/4 cup water or coconut water

Preparation Steps:
In a blender, puree the mangoes, lime juice, and water until smooth. Pour the mixture into a shallow dish and freeze for at least 2 hours. Stir every 30 minutes to create a smooth, sorbet-like texture. Serve chilled.

Nutritional Value (per serving):
Calories: 90 | Protein: 1g | Fat: 0g | Carbohydrates: 23g | Fiber: 3g | Vitamin A: 60% DV | Vitamin C: 80% DV | Iron: 2% DV

78. Banana Oat Cookies

These naturally sweetened banana oat cookies are made with just a few simple ingredients and are a healthy alternative to traditional cookies.

Servings: 12 cookies | **Prep Time**: 5 minutes | **Cooking Time**: 15 minutes

Ingredients:

- 2 ripe bananas, mashed
- 1 1/2 cups rolled oats
- 1/4 cup dark chocolate chips (optional)
- 1/4 cup chopped walnuts (optional)

Preparation Steps:
Preheat the oven to 350°F (175°C). In a large bowl, mix the mashed bananas and oats until combined. Stir in the dark chocolate chips and walnuts if using.

Drop spoonfuls of the mixture onto a lined baking sheet and flatten slightly. Bake for 12-15 minutes, until golden. Let cool before serving.

Nutritional Value (per cookie):
Calories: 80 | Protein: 2g | Fat: 2g | Carbohydrates: 15g | Fiber: 2g | Vitamin A: 2% DV | Iron: 4% DV | Calcium: 2% DV

79. Almond Butter Brownies

These fudgy brownies are made with almond butter and cocoa powder, creating a decadent yet healthy treat that's both gluten-free and naturally sweetened.

Servings: 9 brownies | **Prep Time**: 10 minutes | **Cooking Time**: 20 minutes

Ingredients:

- 1/2 cup almond butter
- 1/4 cup honey or maple syrup
- 1/4 cup unsweetened cocoa powder
- 1 egg
- 1/2 tsp vanilla extract
- 1/4 tsp baking soda

Preparation Steps:
Preheat the oven to 350°F (175°C) and grease an 8x8-inch baking pan. In a bowl, mix the almond butter, honey, cocoa powder, egg, vanilla extract, and baking soda until smooth. Pour the batter into the prepared pan and bake for 18-20 minutes, or until a toothpick comes out clean. Let cool before slicing into squares.

Nutritional Value (per brownie):
Calories: 180 | Protein: 5g | Fat: 12g | Carbohydrates: 15g | Fiber: 3g | Iron: 8% DV | Calcium: 4% DV

80. Pears Poached in Red Wine

This elegant dessert features pears poached in spiced red wine, creating a flavorful and naturally sweet treat that's perfect for special occasions.

Servings: 4 | **Prep Time**: 10 minutes | **Cooking Time**: 25 minutes

Ingredients:

- 4 ripe pears, peeled and cored
- 2 cups red wine
- 1/4 cup honey
- 1 cinnamon stick
- 2 cloves

Preparation Steps:
In a large saucepan, combine the red wine, honey, cinnamon stick, and cloves. Bring to a simmer over medium heat. Add the pears and poach for 20-25 minutes, turning occasionally, until the pears are tender. Remove the pears and let the sauce reduce for an additional 5 minutes. Serve the pears drizzled with the red wine reduction.

Nutritional Value (per serving):
Calories: 220 | Protein: 1g | Fat: 0g | Carbohydrates: 40g | Fiber: 5g | Vitamin C: 6% DV | Iron: 6% DV | Calcium: 2% DV

Chapter 9: Super-Easy Dinners for Busy Weeknights

81. One-Pan Lemon Garlic Chicken with Vegetables

This easy one-pan dish features tender lemon-garlic chicken and roasted vegetables for a quick and nutritious dinner.

Servings: 4 | **Prep Time**: 10 minutes | **Cooking Time**: 30 minutes

Ingredients:

- 4 boneless, skinless chicken breasts
- 2 tbsp olive oil
- 3 cloves garlic, minced
- Juice of 1 lemon
- 1 tsp dried oregano
- 1 zucchini, sliced
- 2 carrots, sliced
- 1 red bell pepper, chopped
- Salt and pepper to taste

Preparation Steps:
Preheat the oven to 400°F (200°C). In a small bowl, whisk together olive oil, garlic, lemon juice, oregano, salt, and pepper. Toss the chicken breasts and vegetables with the mixture and spread them on a sheet pan. Roast for 25-30 minutes, until the chicken is cooked through and the vegetables are tender. Serve hot.

Nutritional Value (per serving):
Calories: 280 | Protein: 30g | Fat: 12g | Carbohydrates: 15g | Fiber: 4g | Vitamin A: 90% DV | Vitamin C: 60% DV | Iron: 10% DV

82. Shrimp & Veggie Stir-Fry with Rice

This quick stir-fry combines shrimp and colorful vegetables served over rice, making it a perfect weeknight meal.

Servings: 4 | **Prep Time**: 10 minutes | **Cooking Time**: 15 minutes

Ingredients:

- 1 lb shrimp, peeled and deveined
- 1 tbsp olive oil
- 1 red bell pepper, sliced
- 1 zucchini, sliced
- 1 cup broccoli florets
- 2 cloves garlic, minced
- 2 tbsp soy sauce
- 1 tbsp sesame oil
- 2 cups cooked rice

Preparation Steps:
Heat olive oil in a large skillet or wok over medium heat. Add the shrimp and cook for 2-3 minutes until pink, then remove and set aside. In the same skillet, stir-fry the bell pepper, zucchini, and broccoli for 5 minutes. Add the garlic, soy sauce, and sesame oil, then stir in the shrimp. Serve the stir-fry over cooked rice.

Nutritional Value (per serving):
Calories: 320 | Protein: 25g | Fat: 10g | Carbohydrates: 30g | Fiber: 5g | Vitamin C: 70% DV | Iron: 15% DV | Calcium: 10% DV

83. Quinoa & Spinach Stuffed Peppers

These colorful bell peppers are filled with a nutritious mixture of quinoa, spinach, and vegetables, making for a healthy and satisfying dinner.

Servings: 4 | **Prep Time**: 15 minutes | **Cooking Time**: 30 minutes

Ingredients:

- 4 large bell peppers, tops removed and seeds scooped out
- 1 cup quinoa, cooked
- 1 cup spinach, chopped
- 1/2 cup diced tomatoes
- 1/4 cup feta cheese (optional)
- 1 tsp oregano

- Salt and pepper to taste

Preparation Steps:
Preheat the oven to 375°F (190°C). In a bowl, combine cooked quinoa, spinach, diced tomatoes, feta (if using), oregano, salt, and pepper. Stuff the bell peppers with the quinoa mixture and place them in a baking dish. Bake for 25-30 minutes, until the peppers are tender. Serve warm.

Nutritional Value (per serving):
Calories: 250 | Protein: 8g | Fat: 8g | Carbohydrates: 35g | Fiber: 6g | Vitamin A: 60% DV | Vitamin C: 120% DV | Iron: 10% DV

84. Sheet Pan Salmon with Asparagus

This simple and healthy sheet pan dinner features roasted salmon and asparagus, perfect for a quick and nutritious meal.

Servings: 4 | **Prep Time**: 5 minutes | **Cooking Time**: 15 minutes

Ingredients:

- 4 salmon fillets (4-6 oz each)
- 1 bunch asparagus, trimmed
- 2 tbsp olive oil
- 1 lemon, sliced
- 2 cloves garlic, minced
- Salt and pepper to taste

Preparation Steps:
Preheat the oven to 400°F (200°C). Arrange the salmon fillets and asparagus on a sheet pan. Drizzle with olive oil, sprinkle with garlic, and season with salt and pepper. Top with lemon slices and roast for 12-15 minutes, until the salmon is flaky and cooked through. Serve hot.

Nutritional Value (per serving):
Calories: 350 | Protein: 30g | Fat: 20g | Carbohydrates: 5g | Fiber: 3g | Vitamin A: 10% DV | Vitamin C: 20% DV | Calcium: 4% DV

85. Zucchini Noodle Alfredo with Grilled Chicken

A low-carb alternative to traditional pasta, this zucchini noodle Alfredo is paired with grilled chicken for a satisfying and healthy dinner.

Servings: 4 | **Prep Time**: 10 minutes | **Cooking Time**: 15 minutes

Ingredients:

- 4 boneless, skinless chicken breasts
- 4 medium zucchinis, spiralized
- 1/2 cup Parmesan cheese, grated
- 1/2 cup heavy cream or almond milk
- 2 cloves garlic, minced
- 2 tbsp olive oil
- Salt and pepper to taste

Preparation Steps:
Grill the chicken breasts for 5-6 minutes per side, until fully cooked, then slice. In a large skillet, heat olive oil over medium heat and sauté the garlic for 1 minute. Add the heavy cream, Parmesan cheese, salt, and pepper, stirring until smooth. Toss the zucchini noodles in the sauce and cook for 2-3 minutes until just tender. Serve with grilled chicken slices on top.

Nutritional Value (per serving):
Calories: 350 | Protein: 35g | Fat: 18g | Carbohydrates: 8g | Fiber: 2g | Vitamin C: 20% DV | Calcium: 15% DV | Iron: 8% DV

86. Chickpea & Vegetable Stew

This hearty and healthy chickpea stew is packed with vegetables and warm spices, making it a comforting meal perfect for busy nights.

Servings: 4 | **Prep Time**: 10 minutes | **Cooking Time**: 25 minutes

Ingredients:

- 1 can chickpeas (15 oz), drained and rinsed
- 1 onion, diced

- 2 carrots, sliced
- 1 zucchini, diced
- 2 cloves garlic, minced
- 1 tsp cumin
- 1 tsp paprika
- 1 can diced tomatoes (14 oz)
- 2 cups vegetable broth

Preparation Steps:
In a large pot, heat olive oil over medium heat and sauté the onion, garlic, carrots, and zucchini for 5 minutes until softened. Stir in cumin and paprika, and cook for 1 minute. Add the chickpeas, diced tomatoes, and vegetable broth, and bring to a simmer. Cook for 20 minutes until the vegetables are tender. Serve hot with fresh parsley on top.

Nutritional Value (per serving):
Calories: 220 | Protein: 8g | Fat: 5g | Carbohydrates: 40g | Fiber: 10g | Vitamin A: 100% DV | Vitamin C: 30% DV | Iron: 15% DV

87. Grilled Turkey Burgers with Sweet Potato Fries

These juicy turkey burgers are paired with crispy sweet potato fries for a healthier twist on a classic meal.

Servings: 4 | **Prep Time**: 10 minutes | **Cooking Time**: 25 minutes

Ingredients:

- 1 lb ground turkey
- 1/4 cup breadcrumbs
- 1 egg
- 1 tsp garlic powder
- Salt and pepper to taste
- 2 medium sweet potatoes, cut into fries
- 2 tbsp olive oil
- 4 whole wheat burger buns

Preparation Steps:
Preheat the oven to 400°F (200°C). Toss the sweet potato fries with olive oil,

salt, and pepper, and spread them on a baking sheet. Roast for 20-25 minutes, flipping halfway through. Meanwhile, in a bowl, mix ground turkey, breadcrumbs, egg, garlic powder, salt, and pepper. Form into patties and grill for 5-6 minutes per side. Serve the burgers on whole wheat buns with sweet potato fries on the side.

Nutritional Value (per serving):
Calories: 400 | Protein: 28g | Fat: 15g | Carbohydrates: 45g | Fiber: 6g | Vitamin A: 120% DV | Iron: 15% DV | Calcium: 8% DV

88. Roasted Vegetable & Hummus Wraps

These easy wraps are filled with roasted vegetables and hummus, creating a quick and healthy dinner option.

Servings: 4 | **Prep Time:** 10 minutes | **Cooking Time:** 25 minutes

Ingredients:

- 1 zucchini, sliced
- 1 red bell pepper, sliced
- 1 onion, sliced
- 2 tbsp olive oil
- 4 large whole wheat wraps
- 1/2 cup hummus
- 1/4 cup fresh spinach

Preparation Steps:
Preheat the oven to 400°F (200°C). Toss the zucchini, bell pepper, and onion with olive oil, salt, and pepper. Roast for 20-25 minutes until tender. Spread hummus on each wrap, top with roasted vegetables and fresh spinach, then roll up. Serve immediately.

Nutritional Value (per serving):
Calories: 300 | Protein: 7g | Fat: 12g | Carbohydrates: 40g | Fiber: 8g | Vitamin A: 20% DV | Vitamin C: 60% DV | Iron: 10% DV

89. Spaghetti Squash with Marinara Sauce

A low-carb alternative to traditional pasta, spaghetti squash is paired with marinara sauce for a light yet satisfying dinner.

Servings: 4 | **Prep Time**: 10 minutes | **Cooking Time**: 40 minutes

Ingredients:

- 1 large spaghetti squash
- 2 cups marinara sauce
- 1/4 cup Parmesan cheese (optional)
- 2 tbsp olive oil
- Salt and pepper to taste

Preparation Steps:
Preheat the oven to 400°F (200°C). Cut the spaghetti squash in half, scoop out the seeds, and drizzle with olive oil, salt, and pepper. Place cut-side down on a baking sheet and roast for 35-40 minutes, until tender. Scrape the squash with a fork to create spaghetti-like strands. Serve with marinara sauce and a sprinkle of Parmesan cheese.

Nutritional Value (per serving):
Calories: 220 | Protein: 5g | Fat: 8g | Carbohydrates: 35g | Fiber: 6g | Vitamin A: 10% DV | Vitamin C: 15% DV | Iron: 8% DV

90. Chicken & Broccoli Stir-Fry with Brown Rice

This classic chicken and broccoli stir-fry is served over brown rice, making for a quick, healthy, and delicious dinner.

Servings: 4 | **Prep Time**: 10 minutes | **Cooking Time**: 15 minutes

Ingredients:

- 2 boneless, skinless chicken breasts, sliced
- 2 cups broccoli florets
- 1 onion, sliced
- 2 tbsp soy sauce

- 1 tbsp olive oil
- 1 tsp sesame oil
- 2 cups cooked brown rice

Preparation Steps:
Heat olive oil in a large skillet over medium heat. Add the sliced chicken and cook for 5-6 minutes until browned. Remove the chicken from the skillet and set aside. In the same skillet, stir-fry the broccoli and onion for 4-5 minutes. Add the soy sauce and sesame oil, then return the chicken to the skillet. Toss everything together and serve over cooked brown rice.

Nutritional Value (per serving):
Calories: 350 | Protein: 28g | Fat: 10g | Carbohydrates: 40g | Fiber: 5g | Vitamin C: 60% DV | Iron: 10% DV | Calcium: 6% DV

Chapter 10: Light and Nourishing Salads

91. Spinach & Quinoa Salad with Lemon Dressing

This vibrant salad combines spinach and protein-packed quinoa with a light lemon dressing, making it a perfect, nutrient-dense meal.

Servings: 4 | **Prep Time**: 10 minutes | **Cooking Time**: 15 minutes

Ingredients:

- 1 cup quinoa, cooked and cooled
- 4 cups fresh spinach
- 1/2 cup cherry tomatoes, halved
- 1/4 cup red onion, thinly sliced
- 1/4 cup feta cheese (optional)
- 2 tbsp olive oil
- Juice of 1 lemon
- Salt and pepper to taste

Preparation Steps:
In a large bowl, combine the cooked quinoa, spinach, cherry tomatoes, red onion, and feta cheese. In a small bowl, whisk together the olive oil, lemon juice, salt, and pepper. Pour the dressing over the salad and toss gently to combine. Serve immediately.

Nutritional Value (per serving):
Calories: 220 | Protein: 7g | Fat: 10g | Carbohydrates: 24g | Fiber: 4g | Vitamin C: 40% DV | Calcium: 10% DV | Iron: 15% DV

92. Arugula & Pear Salad with Walnuts

This light and refreshing salad combines peppery arugula, sweet pear slices, and crunchy walnuts, all topped with a simple vinaigrette.

Servings: 4 | **Prep Time**: 10 minutes | **Cooking Time**: None

Ingredients:

- 4 cups fresh arugula
- 2 ripe pears, thinly sliced
- 1/4 cup walnuts, chopped
- 1/4 cup crumbled blue cheese (optional)
- 2 tbsp olive oil
- 1 tbsp balsamic vinegar
- Salt and pepper to taste

Preparation Steps:
In a large bowl, toss together the arugula, pear slices, walnuts, and blue cheese if using. In a small bowl, whisk together the olive oil, balsamic vinegar, salt, and pepper. Drizzle the dressing over the salad and serve.

Nutritional Value (per serving):
Calories: 180 | Protein: 4g | Fat: 12g | Carbohydrates: 18g | Fiber: 4g | Vitamin A: 15% DV | Vitamin C: 10% DV | Calcium: 8% DV

93. Greek Salad with Feta and Olives

This classic Greek salad is loaded with fresh vegetables, briny olives, and tangy feta cheese, dressed with a light olive oil and lemon vinaigrette.

Servings: 4 | **Prep Time**: 10 minutes | **Cooking Time**: None

Ingredients:

- 4 cups romaine lettuce, chopped
- 1 cucumber, diced
- 1/2 cup cherry tomatoes, halved
- 1/4 cup Kalamata olives, pitted
- 1/4 cup feta cheese, crumbled
- 2 tbsp olive oil
- 1 tbsp lemon juice
- Salt and pepper to taste

Preparation Steps:
In a large bowl, combine the lettuce, cucumber, cherry tomatoes, olives, and

feta cheese. In a small bowl, whisk together the olive oil, lemon juice, salt, and pepper. Drizzle the dressing over the salad and toss to combine. Serve chilled.

Nutritional Value (per serving):
Calories: 150 | Protein: 4g | Fat: 12g | Carbohydrates: 8g | Fiber: 3g | Vitamin A: 20% DV | Vitamin C: 15% DV | Iron: 6% DV

94. Cucumber & Tomato Salad with Balsamic Glaze

This simple, fresh salad of cucumbers and tomatoes is drizzled with a rich balsamic glaze for a light yet flavorful dish.

Servings: 4 | **Prep Time**: 5 minutes | **Cooking Time**: None

Ingredients:

- 2 cucumbers, sliced
- 2 large tomatoes, diced
- 2 tbsp balsamic glaze
- 1 tbsp olive oil
- Salt and pepper to taste
- Fresh basil for garnish

Preparation Steps:
In a bowl, combine the sliced cucumbers and diced tomatoes. Drizzle with balsamic glaze and olive oil, then season with salt and pepper. Garnish with fresh basil and serve immediately.

Nutritional Value (per serving):
Calories: 80 | Protein: 1g | Fat: 5g | Carbohydrates: 9g | Fiber: 2g | Vitamin A: 10% DV | Vitamin C: 20% DV | Calcium: 4% DV

95. Grilled Chicken Caesar Salad

This hearty Caesar salad features grilled chicken, crunchy croutons, and a homemade dressing for a light yet satisfying meal.

Servings: 4 | **Prep Time**: 10 minutes | **Cooking Time**: 10 minutes

Ingredients:

- 2 boneless, skinless chicken breasts, grilled and sliced
- 4 cups romaine lettuce, chopped
- 1/4 cup grated Parmesan cheese
- 1/2 cup croutons
- 2 tbsp olive oil
- 1 tbsp lemon juice
- 1 tsp Dijon mustard
- Salt and pepper to taste

Preparation Steps:
In a large bowl, combine the chopped romaine lettuce, Parmesan cheese, and croutons. In a small bowl, whisk together the olive oil, lemon juice, Dijon mustard, salt, and pepper. Drizzle the dressing over the salad and toss to coat. Top with sliced grilled chicken and serve.

Nutritional Value (per serving):
Calories: 280 | Protein: 25g | Fat: 14g | Carbohydrates: 12g | Fiber: 2g | Vitamin A: 50% DV | Calcium: 15% DV | Iron: 8% DV

96. Watermelon & Feta Salad

This refreshing summer salad pairs juicy watermelon with tangy feta cheese and fresh mint, making it a light and delicious meal or side dish.

Servings: 4 | **Prep Time**: 5 minutes | **Cooking Time**: None

Ingredients:

- 4 cups watermelon, cubed
- 1/4 cup feta cheese, crumbled
- 2 tbsp fresh mint, chopped
- 1 tbsp olive oil
- Juice of 1 lime

Preparation Steps:
In a large bowl, combine the watermelon cubes, crumbled feta, and chopped

mint. Drizzle with olive oil and lime juice, and toss gently to combine. Serve chilled.

Nutritional Value (per serving):
Calories: 120 | Protein: 3g | Fat: 6g | Carbohydrates: 16g | Fiber: 1g | Vitamin C: 25% DV | Calcium: 10% DV | Iron: 4% DV

97. Beet & Goat Cheese Salad

This earthy and sweet beet salad is complemented by creamy goat cheese and crunchy walnuts, all drizzled with a balsamic vinaigrette.

Servings: 4 | **Prep Time**: 10 minutes | **Cooking Time**: 30 minutes

Ingredients:

- 4 medium beets, roasted and diced
- 4 cups mixed greens
- 1/4 cup goat cheese, crumbled
- 1/4 cup walnuts, chopped
- 2 tbsp olive oil
- 1 tbsp balsamic vinegar
- Salt and pepper to taste

Preparation Steps:
In a large bowl, combine the roasted beets, mixed greens, goat cheese, and walnuts. In a small bowl, whisk together the olive oil, balsamic vinegar, salt, and pepper. Drizzle the dressing over the salad and toss to combine.

Nutritional Value (per serving):
Calories: 220 | Protein: 5g | Fat: 15g | Carbohydrates: 18g | Fiber: 4g | Vitamin A: 30% DV | Vitamin C: 15% DV | Iron: 10% DV

98. Chickpea & Kale Salad with Tahini Dressing

This hearty and nutritious salad features protein-packed chickpeas and nutrient-rich kale, tossed in a creamy tahini dressing.

Servings: 4 | **Prep Time**: 10 minutes | **Cooking Time**: None

Ingredients:

- 1 can chickpeas (15 oz), drained and rinsed
- 4 cups kale, chopped
- 1/4 cup tahini
- 2 tbsp lemon juice
- 1 tbsp olive oil
- 1 clove garlic, minced
- Salt and pepper to taste

Preparation Steps:
In a large bowl, massage the kale with a drizzle of olive oil until tender. Add the chickpeas. In a small bowl, whisk together the tahini, lemon juice, garlic, salt, and pepper. Drizzle the dressing over the salad and toss to combine.

Nutritional Value (per serving):
Calories: 250 | Protein: 8g | Fat: 14g | Carbohydrates: 26g | Fiber: 8g | Vitamin A: 80% DV | Vitamin C: 70% DV | Iron: 15% DV

99. Apple & Pecan Salad with Maple Vinaigrette

This fall-inspired salad combines crisp apples, toasted pecans, and mixed greens, all drizzled with a sweet maple vinaigrette.

Servings: 4 | **Prep Time**: 10 minutes | **Cooking Time**: None

Ingredients:

- 4 cups mixed greens
- 2 apples, thinly sliced
- 1/4 cup pecans, toasted
- 2 tbsp olive oil
- 1 tbsp maple syrup
- 1 tbsp apple cider vinegar
- Salt and pepper to taste

Preparation Steps:
In a large bowl, combine the mixed greens, apple slices, and toasted pecans. In

a small bowl, whisk together the olive oil, maple syrup, apple cider vinegar, salt, and pepper. Drizzle the dressing over the salad and toss to combine.

Nutritional Value (per serving):
Calories: 180 | Protein: 2g | Fat: 14g | Carbohydrates: 15g | Fiber: 3g | Vitamin A: 20% DV | Vitamin C: 10% DV | Iron: 4% DV

100. Roasted Butternut Squash Salad

This warm salad features roasted butternut squash, tossed with greens, dried cranberries, and a light vinaigrette for a delicious fall meal.

Servings: 4 | **Prep Time**: 10 minutes | **Cooking Time**: 25 minutes

Ingredients:

- 2 cups butternut squash, cubed
- 4 cups mixed greens
- 1/4 cup dried cranberries
- 1/4 cup pumpkin seeds
- 2 tbsp olive oil
- 1 tbsp balsamic vinegar
- Salt and pepper to taste

Preparation Steps:
Preheat the oven to 400°F (200°C). Toss the butternut squash cubes with olive oil, salt, and pepper, and spread them on a baking sheet. Roast for 20-25 minutes until tender. In a large bowl, combine the mixed greens, dried cranberries, and pumpkin seeds. Add the roasted squash and drizzle with balsamic vinegar. Toss to combine and serve.

Nutritional Value (per serving):
Calories: 220 | Protein: 4g | Fat: 10g | Carbohydrates: 30g | Fiber: 6g | Vitamin A: 150% DV | Vitamin C: 40% DV | Iron: 8% DV

Chapter 12: Bonus Recipes for Special Occasions

101. Dark Chocolate Dipped Strawberries

These elegant and easy-to-make dark chocolate-dipped strawberries are perfect for special occasions, offering a delightful balance of fresh fruit and rich chocolate.

Servings: 4 | **Prep Time**: 10 minutes | **Cooking Time**: 5 minutes

Ingredients:

- 12 large strawberries, washed and dried
- 1/2 cup dark chocolate chips
- 1 tsp coconut oil (optional)

Preparation Steps:
Melt the dark chocolate chips in a microwave or over a double boiler, stirring until smooth. Add the coconut oil for extra shine if desired. Dip each strawberry into the melted chocolate, allowing any excess to drip off. Place the dipped strawberries on a parchment-lined baking sheet and refrigerate for 10-15 minutes to set. Serve chilled.

Nutritional Value (per serving):
Calories: 140 | Protein: 1g | Fat: 8g | Carbohydrates: 18g | Fiber: 3g | Vitamin C: 70% DV | Iron: 6% DV | Calcium: 2% DV

102. Almond & Coconut Cake

This moist and flavorful almond and coconut cake is naturally sweetened and perfect for celebrations, offering a rich texture with a nutty flavor.

Servings: 8 | **Prep Time**: 15 minutes | **Cooking Time**: 35 minutes

Ingredients:

- 1 1/2 cups almond flour
- 1/2 cup shredded coconut
- 1/4 cup honey or maple syrup
- 3 large eggs
- 1/4 cup coconut oil, melted
- 1 tsp vanilla extract
- 1 tsp baking powder

Preparation Steps:
Preheat the oven to 350°F (175°C) and grease an 8-inch cake pan. In a bowl, whisk together the almond flour, shredded coconut, and baking powder. In a separate bowl, mix the eggs, honey, coconut oil, and vanilla extract. Combine the wet and dry ingredients, stirring until smooth. Pour the batter into the prepared cake pan and bake for 30-35 minutes, or until a toothpick comes out clean. Let the cake cool before serving.

Nutritional Value (per serving):
Calories: 250 | Protein: 7g | Fat: 18g | Carbohydrates: 15g | Fiber: 4g | Vitamin E: 10% DV | Iron: 8% DV | Calcium: 6% DV

103. Homemade Cashew Ice Cream with Honey

This creamy homemade cashew ice cream is naturally sweetened with honey, creating a rich and indulgent dessert that's perfect for special occasions.

Servings: 4 | **Prep Time**: 10 minutes | **Cooking Time**: None (freeze for 4 hours)

Ingredients:

- 1 cup raw cashews, soaked overnight
- 1/2 cup coconut milk
- 1/4 cup honey
- 1 tsp vanilla extract
- Pinch of sea salt

Preparation Steps:
Drain and rinse the soaked cashews. In a blender, combine the cashews, coconut milk, honey, vanilla extract, and sea salt. Blend until smooth and

creamy. Pour the mixture into a freezer-safe container and freeze for at least 4 hours, stirring occasionally to break up any ice crystals. Serve when fully frozen.

Nutritional Value (per serving):
Calories: 300 | Protein: 5g | Fat: 20g | Carbohydrates: 28g | Fiber: 2g | Vitamin E: 6% DV | Iron: 10% DV | Calcium: 4% DV

30-Day Meal Plan

This 30-day meal plan incorporates a variety of recipes from the book, balancing nutrition, flavor, and convenience to help you stay energized and healthy. Each day features breakfast, lunch, dinner, and a snack.

Week 1

Day 1

- **Breakfast**: Almond Flour Pancakes with Chia Seeds (Recipe 23)
- **Lunch**: Chickpea & Kale Salad with Tahini Dressing (Recipe 98)
- **Dinner**: One-Pan Lemon Garlic Chicken with Vegetables (Recipe 81)
- **Snack**: Roasted Almond & Cranberry Trail Mix (Recipe 51)

Day 2

- **Breakfast**: Scrambled Eggs with Spinach & Smoked Salmon (Recipe 21)
- **Lunch**: Greek Salad with Feta and Olives (Recipe 93)
- **Dinner**: Quinoa & Spinach Stuffed Peppers (Recipe 83)
- **Snack**: Baked Apple Chips (Recipe 54)

Day 3

- **Breakfast**: Overnight Oats with Berries and Flaxseeds (Recipe 24)
- **Lunch**: Watermelon & Feta Salad (Recipe 96)
- **Dinner**: Shrimp & Veggie Stir-Fry with Rice (Recipe 82)
- **Snack**: Dark Chocolate Dipped Strawberries (Recipe 101)

Day 4

- **Breakfast**: Apple Cinnamon Quinoa Breakfast Bowl (Recipe 25)
- **Lunch**: Roasted Vegetable & Hummus Wraps (Recipe 88)
- **Dinner**: Sheet Pan Salmon with Asparagus (Recipe 84)
- **Snack**: Energy Balls with Peanut Butter and Flaxseeds (Recipe 58)

Day 5

- **Breakfast**: Smoothie: Spinach & Pineapple Smoothie (Recipe 61)
- **Lunch**: Spinach & Quinoa Salad with Lemon Dressing (Recipe 91)
- **Dinner**: Zucchini Noodle Alfredo with Grilled Chicken (Recipe 85)
- **Snack**: Greek Yogurt with Honey and Berries (Recipe 60)

Day 6

- **Breakfast**: Veggie Omelet with Mushrooms and Peppers (Recipe 22)
- **Lunch**: Beet & Goat Cheese Salad (Recipe 97)
- **Dinner**: Chickpea & Vegetable Stew (Recipe 86)
- **Snack**: Homemade Granola Bars with Oats and Dates (Recipe 52)

Day 7

- **Breakfast**: Protein-Packed Banana Oat Muffins (Recipe 30)
- **Lunch**: Roasted Butternut Squash Salad (Recipe 100)
- **Dinner**: Grilled Turkey Burgers with Sweet Potato Fries (Recipe 87)
- **Snack**: Chia Seed Pudding with Mango (Recipe 56)

Week 2

Day 8

- **Breakfast**: Almond Butter & Banana Toast (custom variation on Whole Grain Toast with Avocado and Hemp Seeds, Recipe 26)
- **Lunch**: Cucumber & Tomato Salad with Balsamic Glaze (Recipe 94)
- **Dinner**: One-Pot Chicken & Vegetable Stew (Recipe 38)
- **Snack**: Mango Sorbet with Lime (Recipe 77)

Day 9

- **Breakfast**: Berry & Almond Milk Smoothie (Recipe 62)
- **Lunch**: Greek Yogurt Parfait (Recipe 73)
- **Dinner**: Spaghetti Squash with Marinara Sauce (Recipe 89)

- **Snack**: Roasted Beet and Arugula Salad (Recipe 50)

Day 10

- **Breakfast**: Spinach & Egg Breakfast Muffins (Recipe 9)
- **Lunch**: Apple & Pecan Salad with Maple Vinaigrette (Recipe 99)
- **Dinner**: Grilled Chicken Caesar Salad (Recipe 95)
- **Snack**: Dark Chocolate Almond Bark (Recipe 59)

Day 11

- **Breakfast**: Smoothie: Banana & Peanut Butter Protein Smoothie (Recipe 67)
- **Lunch**: Arugula & Pear Salad with Walnuts (Recipe 92)
- **Dinner**: Quinoa & Roasted Veggie Bowl (Recipe 41)
- **Snack**: Carrot Cake Energy Bites (Recipe 76)

Day 12

- **Breakfast**: Almond Flour Pancakes with Chia Seeds (Recipe 23)
- **Lunch**: Cucumber & Hummus Bites (Recipe 55)
- **Dinner**: Grilled Shrimp with Garlic and Lemon Zest (Recipe 36)
- **Snack**: Baked Sweet Potato with Almond Butter & Cinnamon (Recipe 6)

Day 13

- **Breakfast**: Smoothie: Avocado & Coconut Milk Smoothie (Recipe 69)
- **Lunch**: Spinach & Quinoa Salad with Lemon Dressing (Recipe 91)
- **Dinner**: Roasted Eggplant & Hummus Wraps (Recipe 37)
- **Snack**: Fruit Salad with Mint and Lime (Recipe 53)

Day 14

- **Breakfast**: Scrambled Eggs with Spinach & Smoked Salmon (Recipe 21)
- **Lunch**: Chickpea & Kale Salad with Tahini Dressing (Recipe 98)
- **Dinner**: Grilled Turkey Burgers with Sweet Potato Fries (Recipe 87)

- **Snack**: Almond & Coconut Bliss Balls (Recipe 75)

Week 3

Day 15

- **Breakfast**: Overnight Oats with Berries and Flaxseeds (Recipe 24)
- **Lunch**: Chickpea & Vegetable Stew (Recipe 86)
- **Dinner**: Roasted Vegetable & Hummus Wraps (Recipe 88)
- **Snack**: Greek Yogurt with Honey and Berries (Recipe 60)

Day 16

- **Breakfast**: Smoothie: Green Detox Juice with Cucumber and Apple (Recipe 63)
- **Lunch**: Greek Salad with Feta and Olives (Recipe 93)
- **Dinner**: Zucchini Noodles with Pesto (Recipe 45)
- **Snack**: Roasted Almond & Cranberry Trail Mix (Recipe 51)

Day 17

- **Breakfast**: Chia Seed Pudding with Mango (Recipe 56)
- **Lunch**: Spinach & Quinoa Salad with Lemon Dressing (Recipe 91)
- **Dinner**: Spaghetti Squash with Marinara Sauce (Recipe 89)
- **Snack**: Banana Oat Cookies (Recipe 78)

Day 18

- **Breakfast**: Almond Butter Pancakes with Chia Seeds (Recipe 23)
- **Lunch**: Grilled Chicken Caesar Salad (Recipe 95)
- **Dinner**: Quinoa & Spinach Stuffed Peppers (Recipe 83)
- **Snack**: Chia Seed Pudding with Berries (Recipe 74)

Day 19

- **Breakfast**: Smoothie: Turmeric & Coconut Smoothie (Recipe 66)
- **Lunch**: Watermelon & Feta Salad (Recipe 96)
- **Dinner**: Chickpea & Vegetable Stew (Recipe 86)
- **Snack**: Carrot Cake Energy Bites (Recipe 76)

Day 20

- **Breakfast**: Veggie Omelet with Mushrooms and Peppers (Recipe 22)
- **Lunch**: Beet & Goat Cheese Salad (Recipe 97)
- **Dinner**: Grilled Turkey Burgers with Sweet Potato Fries (Recipe 87)
- **Snack**: Almond Butter Brownies (Recipe 79)

Day 21

- **Breakfast**: Spinach & Pineapple Smoothie (Recipe 61)
- **Lunch**: Cucumber & Tomato Salad with Balsamic Glaze (Recipe 94)
- **Dinner**: Sheet Pan Salmon with Asparagus (Recipe 84)
- **Snack**: Mango Sorbet with Lime (Recipe 77)

Week 4

Day 22

- **Breakfast**: Apple Cinnamon Oatmeal (Recipe 8)
- **Lunch**: Arugula & Pear Salad with Walnuts (Recipe 92)
- **Dinner**: One-Pot Chicken & Vegetable Stew (Recipe 38)
- **Snack**: Energy Balls with Peanut Butter and Flaxseeds (Recipe 58)

Day 23

- **Breakfast**: Scrambled Eggs with Spinach & Smoked Salmon (Recipe 21)
- **Lunch**: Chickpea & Kale Salad with Tahini Dressing (Recipe 98)
- **Dinner**: Grilled Shrimp with Garlic and Lemon Zest (Recipe 36)
- **Snack**: Homemade Granola Bars with Oats and Dates (Recipe 52)

Day 24

- **Breakfast**: Smoothie: Watermelon & Mint Smoothie (Recipe 65)
- **Lunch**: Spinach & Quinoa Salad with Lemon Dressing (Recipe 91)

- **Dinner**: Quinoa & Roasted Veggie Bowl (Recipe 41)
- **Snack**: Dark Chocolate Dipped Strawberries (Recipe 101)

Day 25

- **Breakfast**: Protein-Packed Banana Oat Muffins (Recipe 30)
- **Lunch**: Greek Salad with Feta and Olives (Recipe 93)
- **Dinner**: Roasted Butternut Squash Salad (Recipe 100)
- **Snack**: Baked Apple Chips (Recipe 54)

Day 26

- **Breakfast**: Veggie Omelet with Mushrooms and Peppers (Recipe 22)
- **Lunch**: Beet & Goat Cheese Salad (Recipe 97)
- **Dinner**: Grilled Chicken Caesar Salad (Recipe 95)
- **Snack**: Almond & Coconut Cake (Recipe 102)

Day 27

- **Breakfast**: Smoothie: Banana & Peanut Butter Protein Smoothie (Recipe 67)
- **Lunch**: Chickpea & Vegetable Stew (Recipe 86)
- **Dinner**: Roasted Eggplant & Hummus Wraps (Recipe 37)
- **Snack**: Homemade Cashew Ice Cream with Honey (Recipe 103)

Day 28

- **Breakfast**: Smoothie: Tropical Fruit Juice with Mango and Passion Fruit (Recipe 70)
- **Lunch**: Spinach & Quinoa Salad with Lemon Dressing (Recipe 91)
- **Dinner**: Zucchini Noodle Alfredo with Grilled Chicken (Recipe 85)
- **Snack**: Greek Yogurt Parfait (Recipe 73)

Day 29

- **Breakfast**: Scrambled Eggs with Spinach & Smoked Salmon (Recipe 21)
- **Lunch**: Chickpea & Kale Salad with Tahini Dressing (Recipe 98)

- **Dinner**: One-Pan Lemon Garlic Chicken with Vegetables (Recipe 81)
- **Snack**: Carrot Cake Energy Bites (Recipe 76)

Day 30

- **Breakfast**: Smoothie: Berry & Almond Milk Smoothie (Recipe 62)
- **Lunch**: Arugula & Pear Salad with Walnuts (Recipe 92)
- **Dinner**: Spaghetti Squash with Marinara Sauce (Recipe 89)
- **Snack**: Almond Butter Brownies (Recipe 79)

Conclusion

Final Thoughts on Sustainable Health through Nutrition

As you've seen throughout this book, nutrition plays a fundamental role in shaping your health, energy levels, and overall well-being. By incorporating nutrient-dense, whole foods into your daily life and avoiding heavily processed alternatives, you can not only nourish your body but also take control of your long-term health. Sustainable health is not just about one-time changes; it's about making mindful decisions that become lifelong habits. The recipes and tips shared here are designed to make that journey easier and more enjoyable, without sacrificing flavor or satisfaction.

From nutrient-packed smoothies and salads to hearty, balanced dinners, these meals provide a framework for a lifestyle that supports vitality, energy, and longevity. Whether you are cooking for yourself, your family, or a special occasion, you now have the tools to make thoughtful choices that align with your health goals.

How to Continue Your Journey

Your journey towards better health through nutrition doesn't end here. Consider this book a stepping stone to deeper exploration of how food impacts your body and your life. Continue experimenting with the recipes, adjusting them to fit your preferences, and incorporating new ingredients that inspire you. Stay curious, keep learning, and remain open to adjusting your habits as your body and lifestyle evolve.

Remember, small, consistent changes over time create lasting results. Keep seeking balance, listening to your body, and finding joy in the process of preparing and enjoying nutritious meals. Stay connected to your goals, and you'll find that the benefits of sustained health through nutrition go far beyond the plate—they enrich every aspect of your life.

Let this be just the beginning of a lifelong journey toward better health, greater energy, and true well-being.

Made in the USA
Monee, IL
02 January 2025

75816521R00057